From Jerr

All the Fulness

David Campbell

All the Fulness

David Campbell

Copyright ©, 2016
Jane N. Turley, Gordon P. Campbell

Reprinted in 2017

All rights reserved

ISBN-10: 1974504603
ISBN-13: 9781974504602

Printed in the U.S.A.

To all who love the Truth

God Bless You.

[signature] 9-14-2017

Son of the author
Gordon P. Campbell

Thank you

The penning of a book is an arduous and time-consuming task that requires the cooperation and patient understanding of those close to the author. Without the encouragement and gentle prodding of my dear wife Jean, this task would have never known completion. I am also most indebted to my daughter-in-law Grace who so kindly applied her typing skills to my hand-written drafts. Special thanks also goes to Missionary Wayne Nigh, who in 1973 convinced me that I should and could accomplish such an assignment as authoring this book. But, the greatest acknowledgement of all is reserved for the Almighty God, without whose help, all is impossible.

CONTENTS

Foreword	11
Introduction	13
1. That There Is One God	17
2. That Jesus Is God	30
3. That Jesus Is the Son	77
4. That Jesus Is the Father	96
5. That Jesus Is the Holy Spirit	123
6. Additional Evidence	139
Appendix I Thus Saith the Jehovah's Witnesses	163
Appendix II A Nineteenth Century Testimony	167

Unless otherwise indicated, all scriptural references quoted in this book are taken from the King James Version of the Bible.

FOREWORD

You may never have the privilege of becoming personally acquainted with David Campbell as I have, but after reading *All the Fulness*, you will gain an insight into the character and nature of this man of God. He is a lover of the Truth, and vitally concerned about the souls of men. He is thorough, dedicated, and untiring in his search for the anointing of God. He has allowed God to use him in a mighty way in the writing of this much-needed book.

I have had the pleasure of working with David Campbell in the various phases of the Gospel work for the past twenty years. I have often heard Pastor Campbell preach under the anointing of the Holy Spirit, and observed as the altars would fill with hungry seekers who had been touched by the Word of God as presented by this man. I have seen bodies completely healed as he would lay hands on the believer and pray the prayer of faith in the Name of Jesus. I have seen demons cast out as this Godly preacher allowed the Spirit to use him to defeat the powers of evil.

As I passed through the pages of this manuscript,

upon the request of the author, it seemed that I could almost hear the voice of Elijah reverberating down through the corridors of time. . ."How long halt ye between two opinions?" It is quite obvious that a man cannot hold two opinions concerning the Godhead—neither can he be neutral. But, in a matter of such tremendous importance, it is imperative that a man hold the one and only **correct** opinion.

All the Fulness will be but a short time in your hands when you will acknowledge how scripturally and carefully the subject has been prepared and presented. I urge you to study it with an open heart, confirming the material presented with your own Bible. Above all, allow the Holy Spirit to "guide you into all truth."

This generation, more than any before it, needs men and women who are so in love with the Truth that they will not fear to raise their voices against the flood tides of scriptural inaccuracies and outright heresies. David Campbell is such a man.

As you read this book you will surely be blessed and enlightened as your understanding of the Godhead becomes more clearly focused. Your love and appreciation of Jesus is sure to multiply as you become totally aware that *All the Fulness* dwells bodily in the person of Jesus Christ.

Mervyn D. Miller

INTRODUCTION

The Scriptures declare clearly and in undeniable language that there is only one God. In Deuteronomy 6:4, we find: "Hear O Israel: The Lord our God is one Lord." There is no arguing the fact—the Bible plainly states, with not one exception, that the Lord our God is ONE! Chapter One of this book will be devoted to a scriptural proof that this statement is indeed true.

POLYTHEISM AND MONOTHEISM

The term polytheism simply means the belief in and the worship of a multiplicity of gods. Monotheism, on the other hand, refers to the belief in and the worship of only one god. Trinitarians are offended if they are referred to as being polytheistic, yet they maintain a belief in three distinct persons in the one God. The Jews, on the other hand, have consistently rejected the "one in three" idea, and are incorrigible in their stand that the Old Testament presents the Lord Jehovah as **ONE,** absolutely and completely. Some of the verses that they produce, such as Isaiah 43:10, 11 and Isaiah 44:6, are most convincing to the unbiased and unpreconceived mind.

Many books, both great and small, have been written on the subject of the Godhead, and many may feel that all that is to be said on this vital subject has already been written. For, down through the annals of Church History, leading theologians such as Luther, Calvin, Wesley, Cranmer, Finney, Spurgeon, Hodge, Boettner, Berkhof, and Brumbach, who were all convinced Trinitarians, have included in their voluminous works very dogmatic statements supporting the trinity. They taught, and their followers imbibed—most without bothering to question the scriptural validity of what they were being taught.

However, the amount of material written in support of the unity and absolute Oneness of God is still quite small. In comparison to the pro-trinitarian works, very little has been written to defend the truth of God's Word which states unequivocally that there are three manifestations of the One God to His people, and not three distinct persons who are always in absolute and undisputed harmony. There still remains much to be written by those who maintain a belief in the Oneness of God. It will be my purpose in this book to assist in bridging this gap which has existed far too long. My sincere desire is that through the pages of this volume, honest hearts will be brought to dwell on the many and varied ramifications of this great theme—THE ONENESS OF GOD.

D. Campbell

1

THAT THERE IS ONE GOD

Well over half a century ago Sir James Frazer wrote a book entitled *The Golden Bough* which was hailed by the Bible critics and modernists of the day. In this book on religion and magic, Frazer presented the idea that religion had evolved. He claimed that just as man had evolved from a primeval state to his present being, so had religion evolved from a very crude and rudimentary polytheistic belief to a very sophisticated and refined form of monotheism. By one stroke of the pen Sir James Frazer attempted to obviate the fall of man, the Creation narrative, the authenticity of the Word of God, and the need for a Savior. (See pages 91 and 92 of *The Golden Bough*.) Of course the evolutionists in their belief of the survival of the fittest, and the free thinkers in their denial of God, grabbed the book with both hands and proclaimed it a literary masterpiece in its day.

The subject was far from closed, however, as several professional men who avowed a belief in God set out to refute the contentions of Frazer. One of these men who got to work was a Professor Schmidt, who proved conclusively, by extensive research in a number of countries, that the up-to-date evidences from the most ancient sources proved that mankind, from his earliest, was monotheistic, worshipping one God. Schmidt further proved that it was only later that the inhabitants of these countries degenerated into the worship of a plurality of gods. As the centuries rolled their course, some of these people returned to the worship of the One True God.

This is exactly the way in which the Bible presents it: That man, earliest man, worshipped the One God. Later, however, man fell into the worship of many gods. This continued until God raised up a man (Abraham) and a nation (Israel) to re-educate the world in the worshipping of the One True Living God. Along with true worship of one God, came obedience to His Word.

Along with Schmidt, several noted archeologist began working in an attempt to prove the validity of the Bible from cover to cover. They too were able to prove the verity of the biblical account of montheism. Archibald H. Sayce, Professor of Assyriology, stated that as a former Bible critic, he had had many doubts as to the full authenticity of the Bible until the archeologist' spades began to unearth undeniable evidence. "Then," he said, "all my doubts and criticisms vanished like bubbles in the air."

When we think of men like Sir Frederick Kenyon, Sir Leonard Woolley, Sir Charles Marston, Dr. Langdon, Professor Albright, and many others, all eminent men in the field of Biblical Archeology, who have uncovered the evidences for the historicity, authenticity, and accuracy of the Bible, we can thank God with the Apostle Paul, and say, "If God be for us, who can be against us?" Sir Frederick Kenyon has categorically stated that we can "take the Bible in our hands and say, 'Here we have the Word of God.'"

Several years ago I had the privilege of attending a lecture given by Sir Leonard Wolley at Queen's University in Belfast. The lecture consisted of a special slide presentation giving evidence for the global flood that had originated in Mesopotamia. Without hesitation, Woolley referred to it as "Noah's Flood."

So, the belief in monotheism stands stronger and more robust today than it has in more recent generations. God has vindicated Himself. But, as men have turned from the polytheistic worship of a plurality of heathen gods, have they in reality turned completely to a monotheistic belief? Can we truly say that a belief that demands a triplicity of Gods is truly monotheistic? We think not. For we believe that true monotheism is a belief in one God in absolute purity, not one God in a plurality.

WHAT THE SCRIPTURES SAY

No student of the Bible would attempt to prove that the Word of God ever states that there is more than one God. Therefore, in this first chapter I am on common ground with believers in the trinity. Even in the second chapter, when I take up the proposition, "That Jesus Is God," most all will agree with the majority of what I have to say. It is in the succeeding chapters that the scission will present itself. But for now, let us look at a number of scriptures from different books of the Bible which prove that **God is One.**

All the Fulness

By way of introduction to these scriptures, I quote what C. H. Spurgeon said concerning Revelation 19:9, which reads in part, "And he saith unto me, These are the true sayings of God." Spurgeon said, "If you believe that 'These are the true sayings of God,' you will listen to them with attention, **and judge what you hear from preachers by this infallible standard.** You will receive these words with assurance. This will produce a confidence of understanding. This will produce rest of heart. You will submit with reverence to these words. You will proclaim it with boldness."[1] We do well to remember this statement from Spurgeon as we approach together, "What the Scriptures Say." May God give us confidence of understanding and rest of heart as we proceed to investigate His Word.

In Isaiah 25:1 we read, "O Lord, thou art my God; I will exalt thee, I will praise thy name. . . ." In this passage we see that the God of Isaiah was one God, for he says, "I will exalt **thee**." We also find that His name was one name, for Isaiah says, "I will praise **thy name**." His singularity is thus well demonstrated. Let us remember that the Apostle Thomas (Doubting Thomas) had a similar revelation when, under divine inspiration, he uttered the words recorded in John 20:28—"My Lord and my God." Thomas uttered these words about Jesus, whereas Isaiah exclaimed them about the Jehovah God of the Old Testament. Whereas Thomas said "The Lord of me, and the God of me," Isaiah said, "O Lord, thou art my God." There is, and has always been, only one God. Both these men worshipped Him.

That There Is One God

ANCIENT EGYPT

One of the first and most important lessons which the children of Israel had to learn prior to entering the promised land of Canaan was that God is **One.** They had just left the land of Egypt, a land where they had been enslaved under the cruel yoke of Egyptian bondage. For over four hundred years they had been exposed to the polytheistic worship of idols. In ancient Egypt the worship of many gods was the order of the day, as they paid homage to such gods as Ra, Shu, Nut, Osiris, Isis, Set, Horus, Anubis, Buto, Mut, Ptah, Sekar, Sati, Hapi, Shai, and many, many others. When an idol was built to represent one of these gods, it often had the head of an animal.

Now Israel, who had just left a land infested with paganism, was preparing to enter another land that was filled with idol worship. So, we can readily see the importance that God placed upon Israel receiving a clear revelation that He was the Only God. They were to never allow themselves to be sidetracked into the heathen practice of polytheism, and so the commandment of God was given to them, and it has been resounded down through the ages—"I am the Lord thy God...Thou shalt have no other gods before me...for I the Lord thy God am a jealous God...shewing mercy unto thousands of them that love me, and keep my commandments" (Exodus 20:2-6).

The sixth chapter of Deuteronomy is perhaps even more insistent with these words—"Hear, O Israel: The LORD our God is one LORD: And thou shalt love the LORD thy God with all thine heart, and with all thy soul, and with all thy might. And these words, which I command thee this day, shall be in thine heart: And thou shalt teach them diligently unto thy children, and shalt talk of them when thou sittest in thine house, and when thou walkest by the way, and when thou liest down, and when thou risest up. And thou shalt bind them for a sign upon thine hand, and they shall be as frontlets between thine eyes. And thou shalt write them upon the posts of thy house, and on thy gates. And it shall be, when the LORD thy God shall have brought thee into the land which he sware unto thy fathers, to Abraham, to Isaac, and to Jacob, to give thee great and goodly cities, which thou buildest not, And houses full of all good things, which thou filledst not, and wells digged, which thou diggedst not, vineyards and olive trees, which thou plantedst not; when thou shalt have eaten and be full; Then beware lest thou forget the LORD, which brought thee forth out of the land of Egypt, from the house of bondage. Thou shalt fear the LORD thy God, and serve him, and shalt swear by his name. Ye shall not go after other gods, of the gods of the people which are round about you; (For the LORD thy God is a jealous God among you) lest the anger of the LORD thy God be kindled against thee, and destroy thee from off the face of the earth" (verses 4-15).

God never revealed Himself as a plurality in either the Old Testament or the New Testament. He has always revealed Himself as **ONE**. When Jesus was asked, "Which is the first commandment of all?", he answered, "Hear, O Israel; The Lord our God is one Lord" (Mark 12:28, 29). We can see from this passage of Scripture, as well as those preceding it, that to the people of God, absolute monotheism is a must!

That There Is One God

NO OTHER GOD

In Deuteronomy 32:36-39, we read in part, "For the LORD shall judge his people...And he shall say, Where are their gods, their rock in whom they trusted...See now that I, even I, am he, and there is no god with me:" This statement is absolute, and leaves no room for doubt or supposition. It spells out the deathkneel to those that insist on believing that the Godhead is a committee of three. This verse states that "There Is No God With Me." So, we have no choice but to believe that there is only one God, and that He is absolute and complete in Himself. He needs no counselor, He needs no assistance, and He needs no adjudicator. He is complete and supreme in knowledge and in power, and He filleth all things with His presence.

In Malachi 2:10, the question is asked, "Have we not all one father? hath not one God created us?" On page 930 of Dake's Annotated Reference Bible, Finis J. Dake admits that one God was the Creator, and that He who created us is one. Yet, on this very same page, when dealing with the subject, "Fellow of Jehovah" (Zechariah 13:7), he goes on to say "The Hebrew word for *fellow* is *awmeeth*, which comes from a primitive root meaning to associate with, to have companionship with, to be a comrade with, or to be kindred to another fellow of the same kind and nature." Thus, we are told by Dake that this proves that there is more than one person in the Godhead. According to Dake, this Shepherd mentioned in Zechariah is a fellow-God, **ANOTHER GOD**, a comrade God, an associate God, or a kindred God.

We hate to destroy Mr. Dake's neat system, but he can't have it both ways. Either he believes in one

All the Fulness

God, or he doesn't. Deuteronomy 32:39 says, "I, even I, am he, and there is no god with me." Isaiah 42:8 states, "I am the LORD: that is my name: and my glory will I not give to another." Isaiah 43:11 tells us, "I, even I, am the LORD; and beside me there is no saviour." Verse 15 of that same chapter reads, "I am the LORD, your Holy One, the creator of Israel, your King." In Isaiah 45:21, 22 we find, "Tell ye, and bring them near; yea, let them take counsel together: who hath declared this from ancient time? who hath told it from that time? have not I the LORD? and there is no God else beside me; a just God and a Saviour; there is none beside me. Look unto me, and be ye saved, all the ends of the earth: for I am God, and there is none else."

Mr. Dake has made his mistake through not recognizing the difference between our Lord in His Absolute Deity, and our Lord in His redemptive role. He makes confusion, and not fusion between the supreme deity and the perfect humanity of the Lord Jesus Christ. We cannot believe in a plurality of Gods, such as "Another God," and still profess to believe in one God. To do so is a direct contradiction. So, the Scripture still holds true when it declares, "Hear, O Israel: The LORD our God is one LORD."

According to Dake's interpretation of Zechariah 13:7, there would be two Shepherds—the Father and the Son (See also Psalm 23:1 and John 10:11). But, in Ezekiel 37:24, it is categorically stated that "They all shall have one shepherd." Verse 22 of the same chapter tells us that "One king shall be king to them all." There is but one Chief Shepherd of the sheep, and His name is Jesus (I Peter 5:4). We are reminded in Zechariah 14:9 that, "The LORD shall be king over all the earth: in that day shall there be one LORD, and

That There Is One God

his name one." One God with one name. Think of that—His very name shall be one!

In Matthew 19:17 the Lord Jesus plainly declared that, "There is none good but one, that is, God." It is clearly seen that He was speaking of the Father in this passage. So, if we do not admit that Jesus is the Father, then we must admit that Jesus is not good. We will touch on this point more fully in a later chapter. Matthew 23:9 tells us, "For one is your Father, which is in heaven." We are told in I Corinthians 8:4, "There is none other God but one." Two verses later (I Corinthians 8:6) we are told who this God is—"But to us there is but one God, the Father."

How then can we possibly have "Another God?" I Timothy 2:5 further confirms our belief when it states, "For there is one God, and one mediator between God and men, the man Christ Jesus." It is the clear and lucid teaching of **all** Scripture that there is **ONLY ONE GOD!** This fact is unmistakable as we turn the pages of the Holy Writ. God's precious Word is infallible in its pronouncement that **He Is One!**

In Ephesians 4:6 the Apostle Paul says there is, "One God and Father of all, who is above all, and through all, and in you all." In the next chapter of this book, which is entitled "That Jesus Is God," it will be proven from Romans 9:5 that it is Jesus Christ who is above all. And in the fifth chapter, entitled "That Jesus Is The Holy Spirit," it will be shown that *He is* **in** *you all.* For in Colossians 1:27 we find, "Christ in you, the hope of glory." Colossians 3:11 reads, "But Christ is all, and in all." We also find in Ephesians 1:23 that He is, "the fulness of him that filleth all in all." In other words, He is omnipresent. But, getting back to Ephesians 4:6, Paul says that there is, "One God and Father of all." Thus we have one of the greatest

All the Fulness

themes of the Bible—The Oneness of God.

James 2:19 says, "Thou believest that there is one God; thou doest well: the devils also believe, and tremble." This verse only adds to the already established fact that it is of utmost importance that we believe that there is one God without fear or equivocation. The verse goes on to say that not even the demons of hell would dispute the Oneness of God. Yes, we do well to adhere completely to the great tenet of the true Christian religion.

HODGE'S OUTLINES OF THEOLOGY

The Reverend A. A. Hodge, who was the son of the well-known Dr. Charles Hodge of Princeton Theological Seminary, wrote a treatise entitled *Outlines of Theology*. On page 107 and 108 Hodge, who like his father was a Trinitarian, had this to say about the unity of God: "There is only one God to the exclusion of all others...there appears to be a necessity in reason for conceiving of God as one. That which is absolute and infinite cannot but be one and indivisible in essence. If God is not one, then it will necessarily follow that there are more gods than one...The whole Creation, between the outermost range of telescopic and microscopic observation, is manifestly one indivisible system...We have already proved the existence of God from the phenomena of the universe; and we now argue, upon the same principle, that if an effect proves the prior operation of a cause, and if traces of design prove a designer, then singleness of plan and operation in that design and its execution proves that the designer is one...The existence of God is said to be necessary

That There Is One God

because it has its cause from eternity itself. It is the same in all duration and in all space alike.

"It is absurd to conceive of God not existing at any time, or in any portion of space, while all other existence whatsoever, depending upon His mere will, is contingent. But the necessity which is uniform in all times and in every portion of space, is evidently only one and indivisible, and can be the ground of the existence only of One God. The argument is logical, and has been prized highly by many distinguished theologians."[2]

Proponents in the absolute, indivisible, Oneness of God could not have stated this blessed truth more clearly and precisely.

MARK 12:32-34

In this passage of Scripture a scribe is discoursing with Jesus, and has in fact just finished asking Him a question in verse 28—"Which is the first commandment of all?" To this question Jesus replied, "The first of all the commandments is, Hear, O Israel; The Lord our God is one Lord." In verses 32-34 of the same chapter, we read, "And the scribe said unto him, Well, Master, thou hast said the truth: for there is one God; and there is none other but he: And to love him with all the heart, and with all the understanding, and with all the soul, and with all the strength, and to love his neighbour as himself, is more than all whole burnt offerings and sacrifices. And when Jesus saw that he answered discreetly, he said unto him, Thou art not far from the kingdom of God."

Please note with me the words of the scribe as he says, "For there is one God, and there is none other

All the Fulness

but he." This is a further answer to the inconsistencies of Mr. Dake. There is not, as he put it, "Another God," for the Bible plainly states that, "There is one God, and there is none other but he." Notice the use here of the singular personal pronoun. "There is none other but **he.**" "And to love **him** with all the heart."

These references concerning God are related to one singular Being. The scribe was speaking correctly. We, too, do well to make certain that our terminology is correct and scripturally accurate when making reference to God. The word *TRINITY*, to the consternation of many, is not found in the Bible. Terminological inexactitudes may be permissible in some circumstances of life, but not when it comes to Biblical Theology. How can we make a unity into a trinity, and still claim that it is a unity?

THE NATURE OF GOD

This is the most interesting part of our study. In John 4:24 Jesus said to the woman at the well, "God is a Spirit." In I Corinthians 12:13 we read, "For by one Spirit are we all baptized unto one body." Likewise, Ephesians 4:4 tells us that there is one Spirit, and in Hebrews 12:9 we discover that God is the "Father of spirits." God is therefore the self-existing, unchangeable eternal Spirit. A. A. Hodge put it this way; "God...is a personal Spirit, infinite, eternal, self-existent, the first cause of all things, infinitely intelligent, powerful, free of will, righteousness, and benevolent."[3]

He who was the Father of our Lord's humanity was the Spirit of God (Matthew 1:20). And in I

That There Is One God

Corinthians 15:45 we read that Christ was raised from the dead, "a quickening (life-giving) spirit." This is again confirmed by II Corinthians 3:17 which says, "Now the Lord is that Spirit." Therefore, this One God, the great infinitely loving eternal Spirit, has revealed Himself as Father, Son and Holy Spirit, yet remaining one God, one Spirit, who filleth all things. Surely with the hymn writer, we can say, "How Great Thou Art."

As to His eternally divine nature, the Bible reveals that God is a Spirit, and that He is One. A number of other points relative to the attributes and titles of God will be treated in appropriate parts of this book. I refer to such topics as: "Who is the Alpha and Omega of the Scripture—is there one or two?" "Who is the Everlasting Father—is there one or two, and what does the term mean?" "Who is the Ancient Days?" And, "How many Gods will come back when Jesus returns—one or two?"

Therefore, seeing that the whole of Christendom confesses that they believe **God Is One,** we need not pursue this chapter further. The only man who would question the basic proposition that God is One is the pagan worshipper of idols. So, now that we have laid the solid foundation for our study, let us continue.

In Chapter Two we will present for your consideration irrefutable statements, backed by Scripture, pointing to the fact "That Jesus Is God."

---

[1]*My Sermon Notes,* By C. H. Spurgeon, p. 1060
[2]*Outlines of Theology,* By A. A. Hodge, pp. 107, 108
[3]*Ibid,* p. 104

2

THAT JESUS IS GOD

The name Jehovah is a transliteration of the Hebrew name "Yahweh." The divine disclosure of the meaning of this name is "I am that I am." The name expresses self-existence and unchangeableness. In Exodus 3:14 God said unto Moses, "I AM THAT I AM." When the announcement of the birth of Jesus was made, the angel of God said, "And they shall call his name Emmanuel, which being interpreted is, God with us" (Matthew 1:23). When we look at the meaning of Jehovah—"the self-existing, unchangeable I Am," and as we investigate certain scriptures, we can readily see that the Jehovah of the Old Testament is the Jesus of the New Testament.

In the New Testament Jesus is revealed as "the self-existing, unchangeable I Am." He declared Himself to the unbelieving Jews with these words— "Before Abraham was, I am" (John 8:58). A number of other scriptures to which we shall later refer also present Him as the "I Am." In Hebrews 13:8 we read, "Jesus Christ the same yesterday, and today, and for

That Jesus Is God

ever." Thus, we find the self-existing and eternally unchangeable Jehovah of the Old Testament in the person of Jesus Christ in the New Testament. And in Hebrews 1:10-12, we find the following attributed to Jesus: "And, Thou, Lord, in the beginning hast laid the foundation of the earth; and the heavens are the works of thine hands: They shall perish; but thou remainest; and they all shall wax old as doth a garment; And as a vesture shalt thou fold them up, and they shall be changed: but thou art the same, and thy years shall not fail."

Jesus Christ has encased within Himself **ALL** the attributes and the qualities of deity. Colossians 2:9 sums up the true identity of Jesus better than any other scripture when it states, "For in him dwelleth all the fulness of the Godhead bodily." This verse clearly tells us that *It's all in Him.* And if all the fulness of the Godhead is in Jesus, what does that leave for the two remaining members of the trinity (for those that believe that such a relationship exists)? Even those professing to believe in a triplicity of Gods will admit to the omnipotence, omniscience, and omnipresence of the Godhead. How is it possible for three different beings to be all-powerful, all-knowing, and all-present? Common sense itself tells us that this is an impossibility.

In John 14:8,9 we find the following conversation between Jesus and Philip: "Philip saith unto him, Lord, shew us the Father, and it sufficeth us. Jesus saith unto him, Have I been so long time with you, and yet hast thou not known me, Philip? he that hath seen me hath seen the Father; and how sayest thou then, Shew us the Father? In other words, Jesus was saying to Philip, "Why are you looking elsewhere for the Father, Philip? Look at me Philip, and you will see

All the Fulness

the Father." Jesus went on to say in verse eleven of the same chapter, "Believe me that I am in the Father, and the Father in me: or else believe me for the very works' sake."

Adding to the already infallible proof of the absolute and total deity of Jesus Christ is the statement found in Romans 9:5 which reads, "Whose are the fathers, and of whom as concerning the flesh Christ came, who is over all, God blessed for ever. Amen." The word of God states here in an indisputable manner that He who became Christ (Jesus) is God over all. In other words, He who was born in a manger in Bethlehem; He who became the son of a carpenter; He who at the age of twelve astounded the doctors in the temple; He who at the age of thirty began His public ministry; and He who some forty-two months later gave His life on a cross, was not some junior member of a council of gods, but the One and Only God, robed in the flesh of a man. God did not send His son to die on a cross—He came Himself.

FOUR PROOFS OF HIS ABSOLUTE DEITY

At this point in the chapter it seems proper to present four proofs relating to the absolute deity of Jesus. The first proof concerns the incarnation of Jesus. The second proof concerns His absolute deity in relation to His earthly ministry. The third proof concerns the absolute deity of Jesus in relation to His ascension. The fourth proof concerns Jesus' absolute deity in relation to the Second Coming.

That Jesus Is God

HIS ABSOLUTE DEITY RELATIVE TO HIS INCARNATION

In Matthew 1:23 we read, "And they shall call his name Emmanuel, which being interpreted is, God with us." In one simple statement the entire redemptive plan of God is revealed. God will veil Himself in flesh, and visit mankind for a season—until His redemptive purpose is completed. This is a fulfillment of Isaiah 7:14, which prophesies that, "A virgin shall conceive, and bear a son, and shall call his name Immanuel."

In Isaiah 9:6 we find further scripture relating to the incarnation of Jesus. It reads, "For unto us a child is born, unto us a son is given: and the government shall be upon his shoulder: and his name shall be called Wonderful, Counsellor, The mighty God, The everlasting Father, The Prince of Peace." So, we discover that "this Child that is to be born," and "this Son that is to be given," is also "The mighty God," and "The everlasting Father." In His humanity, He was the Child that was born, and the Son that was given. In His deity, He was the mighty God, and the everlasting Father. Jesus was just as much the everlasting Father as He was the Son given. He was not part man and part God, but He was all man and all God. For though He took upon Himself the completeness of humanity, in Him dwelt all the fulness of the Godhead bodily. For, "God was in Christ, reconciling the world unto himself" (II Corinthians 5:19).

Micah 5:2 reads, "But thou, Bethlehem Ephratah, though thou be little among the thousands of Judah, yet out of thee shall he come forth unto me that is to be ruler in Israel; whose goings forth have been from

All the Fulness

of old, from everlasting." Once again, we find that the Babe that was to be born in the manger in Bethlehem was in reality God descending in the form of man.

We now step over into the New Testament where we find, "In the beginning was the Word, and the Word was with God, and the Word was God" (John 1:1). The original Greek text reads thus: "EN ARCHE EN HO LOGOS, KAI HO LOGOS EN PROS TON THEON, KAI THEOS EN HO LOGOS." The last part of the verse, "KAI THEOS EN HO LOGOS," in its literal translation, reads, "And God was the Word." Verse fourteen of the same chapter reads, "And the Word was made flesh, and dwelt among us, (and we beheld his glory, the glory as of the only begotten of the Father,) full of grace and truth." Thus, we find that the Word, which is God, became flesh, which is Jesus. This is in keeping with I Timothy 3:16 which states, "God was manifest in the flesh." Therefore, we find that at the Incarnation, the Absolute Deity became robed in flesh.

In Isaiah 40:3 the prophet foretells of Jesus in saying, "The voice of him that crieth in the wilderness, Prepare ye the way of the LORD, make straight in the desert a highway for out God." In fulfillment of this prophecy, we read the following account in Matthew 3:1-3: "In those days came John the Baptist, preaching in the wilderness of Judaea, And saying, Repent ye: for the kingdom of heaven is at hand. For this is he that was spoken of by the prophet Esaias (Isaiah), saying, The voice of one crying in the wilderness, Prepare ye the way of the Lord, make his paths straight." Once again, the Word of God points with such clarity that the Jehovah of the Old Testament robed Himself in flesh, and became the Jesus of the New Testament. This action was

That Jesus Is God

necessary for the redemption of mankind. Since the Fall of Man had resulted from the fleshly weaknesses of the First Adam, it was necessary for the Second Adam to gain victory over these same fleshly weaknesses in order for redemption to be possible. To truly gain victory over the carnal tendencies of man, Jesus had to be tempted in the manner common to all humanity. The victory was won, and redemption was the result, as the Lamb that was offered for the final sacrifice was without blemish.

Even when the Babe was in her womb, Mary said, "My soul doth magnify the Lord, And my spirit hath rejoiced in God my Saviour" (Luke 1:46, 47). So, under the anointing of God, Mary expressly declared that her Lord and her God was about to become her Savior. These words are so reminiscent of the words of Thomas as he viewed the wounded side and the nail-scarred hands of Jesus—"My Lord and my God." The Apostle Paul sums it up with the words of Titus 2:13 which read, "Looking for that blessed hope, and the glorious appearing of the great God and our Saviour Jesus Christ."

This then is the testimony of the Scripture. Louis Berkhof, an outstanding Presbyterian Bible teacher and commentator, who had a long and distinguished career as a professor of theology at Calvin Theological Seminary in Grand Rapids, makes an interesting statement concerning the Oneness of God. On page 26 of *Summary of Christian Doctrine*, Berkhof makes reference to Psalm 147:5 which says, "Great is our Lord, and of great power: his understanding is infinite." Berkhof's comment is; "The Great God of the Old Testament is the same Great God of the New Testament, and His name is Jesus (Psalm 147:5; Titus 2:13)."

HIS ABSOLUTE DEITY RELATIVE TO HIS EARTHLY MINISTRY

The Gospels, which record the earthly ministry of Jesus, contain numerous scriptures attesting to His absolute deity. One of the first, which is found in Luke 2:32, embraces the words of the aged Jew, Simeon, as he held the baby Jesus in the temple. In speaking of Jesus, Simeon referred to Him as, "A light to lighten the Gentiles, and the glory of thy people Israel." Each time the term "Glory of Israel" (as related to a person) was used in the Old Testament, it referred to the Lord Jehovah. An example of this can be found in Psalm 24:7-10 which says, "Lift up your heads, O ye gates; and be ye lift up, ye everlasting doors; and the King of glory shall come in. Who is the King of glory? The lord strong and mighty, the LORD mighty in battle. Lift up your heads, O ye gates; even lift them up, ye everlasting doors; and the King of glory shall come in. Who is the King of glory? The LORD of hosts, he is the King of glory. Se-lah."

We will return to these scriptures at a later time when dealing with the topic of "His Absolute Deity Relative To His Ascension." In addition to making reference to the earthly ministry of Jesus, they also prophesy of His ascension.

From the preceding scriptures, it becomes quite evident that the "glory of thy people Israel," that Simeon held in the temple, was the same as the "King of glory" mentioned in Psalm 24. He is referred to in Psalm 24:10 as the "LORD of hosts" (Jehovah Sabaoth, a term signifying the great power of Jehovah), while I Timothy 6:14, 15 speaks of Him in the following manner: "...our Lord Jesus Christ: Which in his times he shall shew, who is the blessed

That Jesus Is God

and only Potentate, the King of kings, and Lord of lords."

In Psalm 29:3-5 we read that, "The voice of the LORD is upon the waters; the God of glory thundereth: the LORD is upon many waters. The voice of the LORD is powerful; the voice of the LORD is full of majesty. The voice of the LORD breaketh the cedars; yea, the LORD breaketh the cedars of Lebanon." Verse 10 of the same chapter states, "The LORD sitteth upon the flood; yea, the LORD sitteth King for ever." So, once more we see very clearly that He who sits as King of kings, and He who rules as Lord of lords over all creation, is indeed the "God of glory." Paul refers to Him in I Corinthians 2:8 as the "Lord of glory." Either way, He is "the glory of thy people Israel."

Isaiah 42:8 says, "I am the LORD: that is my name: and my glory will I not give to another. . . ." So, if Jesus is not the Jehovah of the Old Testament, and if He is not the Great I Am, then He can not possibly be "the glory of thy people Israel,," or the "Lord of glory" referred to by Paul. For, we have just read that God will not share His glory with **another.** If we cannot accept the fact that Jesus was indeed God himself manifested in flesh, then we must decide who was lying—Isaiah, Simeon, or Paul.

Isaiah 48:11 repeats the great truth found in Isaiah 8 in saying, "For mine own sake, even for mine own sake, will I do it: for how should my name be polluted? and I will not give my glory unto another." By reading the entire chapter, we discover that God, in speaking of **another**, is referring to anything or anyone, other than the Eternal Jehovah himself, that man may attempt to deify.

It remains a mystery indeed why anyone would

insist on a multiplicity of persons in the Godhead. Isaiah 45:21 states in a manner saturated with clarity and simplicity that, "There is no God else beside me; a just God and a Saviour; there is none beside me." And once again we go to the familiar passage found in Deuteronomy 6:4, which says, "Hear, O Israel: The LORD our God is one LORD." And as if further proof were needed, we go to John 10:30 in which Jesus states, "I and my Father are one." Many Trinitarians sorrowfully admit difficulty in attempting to prove the validity of the trinity. They should not feel too badly, however, for the Bible runs into the same problem.

Ezekiel 8:4 tells us, ". . .behold, the glory of the God of Israel was there. . ." Zechariah 2:5 says, "For I, saith the LORD. . .will be the glory in the midst of her." Yes, according to Scripture, God is "the glory of thy people Israel." But, Simeon spoke these very words about the babe Jesus. Have we any alternative but to admit that Jesus was God manifested in the flesh, and not the number two member of a council of Gods?

Jesus Reveals Himself As Father

The following passage of scripture has already been mentioned, and will be treated again in the chapter entitled "That Jesus Is The Father." But, since it has such a distinctive relationship to the topic we are presently discussing (the earthly ministry of Jesus), we will discuss it here also. In John 14:8, 9 we read, "Philip saith unto him, Lord, shew us the Father, and it sufficeth us. Jesus saith unto him, Have I been so long time with you, and yet hast thou not known me, Philip? he that hath seen me hath seen the Father; and how sayest thou then, Shew us the Father?" Jesus seemed to be saying to Philip, "Why do you look for another? If you have seen me, you have also seen the One who is the Father. Why do you say, 'show us the Father?' How long must I be with you before you recognize the fact that I am both the Father and the Son?"

The Jerusalem Bible translates John 14:8, 9 in the following manner: "Philip said, 'Lord, let us see the Father and then we shall be satisfied.' 'Have I been with you all this time, Philip,' said Jesus to him, 'and you still do not know me? To have seen me is to have seen the Father, so how can you say, Let us see the Father?'"

There were many times in the earthly ministry of Jesus that He revealed Himself as the Father, as well as the Son. Not one statement made by Jesus, or act attributed to Him contradicted the teaching of the Old Testament Scripture concerning the Oneness of God. True to the words of Isaiah, Jesus was a "child born," and a "son given," as well as the "everlasting Father."

Jesus Reveals Himself As The Spirit

In addition to revealing Jesus as the Father, John 14 also reveals Him as the Spirit. In verse 16 Jesus says, "And I will pray the Father, and he shall give you another Comforter, that he may abide with you for ever." Jesus' bodily presence with the disciples in the fleshly form of the Son was temporary. To the carnal minds of these followers, the physical presence of Jesus was very important. As stated in I John 1:1, it was possible for the disciples of Jesus to look upon Him with their eyes, and touch Him with their hands. To men that were familiar only with the tangible, this was a great encouragement. Jesus continued to tell

All the Fulness

them, however, that His stay on earth was but for a while, and then He would leave them. They were not to dispair, however, for He promised to send them another Comforter. This new Comforter would have two distinct advantages over the present one. First, It would be **in** them, and not merely **with** them. Also, It would abide on a permanent basis, rather than a temporary one.

Verses 16 through 18 of this same chapter are most revealing concerning the true identity of the Godhead. In verse 16 Jesus tells the disciples that He will pray to the Father, asking Him to send them another Comforter. Verse 17 describes this Comforter, telling what mankind's reaction will be to Him. Verse 18 states that Jesus, himself, will be the new Comforter. When we add verse 23, which tells us that both the Father and the Son will dwell in the hearts of those that keep the commandments, we have no choice but to admit that Jesus is the Father, the Son, and the Comforter (Holy Ghost).

The Word of God points out in indisputable language that He who was in the world for thirty-three and a half years; He who at that moment was standing with the disciples; He who would soon die on a cross; and He who would a short time later ascend into heaven, would return to them in the form of the Holy Spirit. He would remain with them in that form throughout the Church Age. Perhaps this blessed truth is best summarized by the words of Colossians 1:27 which reads, "To whom God would make known what is the riches of the glory of this mystery among the Gentiles; which is Christ in you, the hope of glory."

Ephesians 3:17 says in part, "That Christ may dwell in your hearts. . . ." In John 17:23 Jesus says, "I

That Jesus Is God

in them, and thou in me." I John 3:24 reads, "And he that keepeth his commandments dwelleth in him, and he in him. And hereby we know that he abideth in us, by the Spirit which he hath given us." Revelation 3:20 says, "Behold, I stand at the door, and knock: If any man hear my voice, and open the door, I will come in to him, and will sup with him, and he with me." And in Matthew 28:20 we find Jesus saying, "Lo, I am with you alway, even unto the end of the world." Keeping these scriptures in mind, it seems quite evident that Jesus and the Holy Spirit are one in the same.

In declaring Jesus to be the Almighty God himself, we are not making a claim that Jesus did not make about Himself. In claiming that Jesus is the Holy Spirit that was sent down to be a Comforter to mankind, we are simply repeating the words that Jesus spoke concerning Himself. There is a much-used statement that seems appropriate to quote at this juncture: "If He is not Lord of all, then He is not Lord at all." If we insist on making the Son one-third of the total Godhead, then we must be content in ascribing to Him only one-third of the power. Thus, He is no longer omnipotent, a quality that the Bible imputes to God.

The Name Revealed

Psalm 22 is a Messianic Psalm. The Messianic Psalms are those which are prophetic in nature, predicting events in the Life of Jesus hundreds of years before His birth in Bethlehem. In Psalm 22:1 we are told the very words Jesus would cry out just prior to His death on Calvary: "My God, my God, why hast thou forsaken me?" To substantiate this, we go to the words of Jesus as recorded in Matthew 27:46: "And

All the Fulness

about the ninth hour Jesus cried out with a loud voice, saying, E-li, E-li, la-ma sa-bach'-tha-ni? that is to say, My God, my God, why hast thou forsaken me?"

Psalm 22:16 describes the details of the death of Jesus in saying, "For dogs have compassed me; the assembly of the wicked have inclosed me: they pierced my hands and my feet." Psalm 22:18 says, "They part my garments among them, and cast lots upon my vesture." We go to Matthew 27:35 and see that this prophecy was fulfilled exactly, as we read, "And they crucified him, and parted his garments, casting lots: that it might be fulfilled which was spoken by the prophet, They parted my garments among them, and upon my vesture did they cast lots."

But there is another prophetic verse in Psalm 22 which is often over-looked. Psalm 22:22 says, "I will declare thy name unto my brethren: in the midst of the congregation will I praise thee." During His earthly ministry, Jesus did exactly that. We find the fulfillment of this particular prophecy in the words of the prayer Jesus uttered in the Garden of Gethesemane. As the Flesh agonized before the Spirit, Jesus prayed, "I have manifested thy name unto the men which thou gavest me out of the world: thine they were, and thou gavest them me; and they have kept thy word" (John 17:6). *The Moffatt Translation* of the verse reads in this manner: "I have made thy name known to the men whom thou hast given to me from the world. . . and they have held to thy word."

Through Jesus, the name of God was made known unto the disciples. Jesus was able to answer the question asked in Proverbs 30:4: "What is his name, and what is his son's name, if thou canst tell?" Can we determine what the name is that is common

That Jesus Is God

to the Father and the Son? Jesus said in John 5:43, "I am come in my Father's name." In Hebrews 1:4 we read, "He hath by inheritance obtained a more excellent name than they."

Referring back to John 17, we find that Jesus bore the name of the Father. Therefore, it is clearly evident that the Father and the Son share a name. What is it? *The Moffatt Translation* of John 17:11, 12 reads in part, "Holy Father, keep them by the power of thy Name which thou hast given me. . . .When I was with them, I kept them by the power of thy Name which thou hast given me."

So we see that Jesus bore the Name that is above every other name (Philippians 2:9-11). It is the name before which every knee must bow. "For there is none other name under heaven given among men, whereby we must be saved" (Acts 4:12). But, when we turn to the pages of the Old Testament, we find these same attributes mentioned, and they always refer to the Jehovah God.

In Isaiah 45:21-23 we read, "There is no God else beside me; a just God and a Saviour; there is none beside me. Look unto me, and be ye saved, all the ends of the earth: for I am God, and there is none else. I have sworn by myself, the word is gone out of my mouth in righteousness, and shall not return, That unto me every knee shall bow, every tongue shall swear." Returning to Philippians 2:10, we find that every knee shall bow at the name of Jesus. In the next verse we find that every tongue shall confess that Jesus Christ is Lord. Can our minds retain any doubt as to the fact that the Father and the Son share the name Jesus? And, since there appears to be only one name in the Godhead, is it possible that there is only one person in the Godhead? Surely this must be the case!

In reading John 17:6, we are led to believe that Jesus had already instructed the disciples concerning the fact that the name (Jesus) which he bore was a name encompassing the entire Deity. It was a name common to the three manifestations of the One God. This was indeed a supreme revelation of the name to mankind. Hence, it is no wonder, and neither should we be surprised to learn, that when Jesus told the disciples in Matthew 28:19 to baptize in the name of the Father, and of the Son, and of the Holy Ghost, they obeyed His commandment by baptizing in the Name of Jesus.

The Bible is not mistaken, and Peter, along with the other Apostles, did not misunderstand or disobey. They understood precisely what Jesus had meant, and they obeyed His baptismal formula "to a tee." This correct mode of baptism was continued for many years in the church before the heretical interpretation of Matthew 28:19 was introduced, causing the main body of the church to initiate a form of baptism that was unscriptural.

Zechariah 11:12, 13

In the foregoing instances, we have been able to establish that the absolute deity of Jesus was revealed through His earthly ministry. Before going to the next section, however, I wish to introduce a few more passages which further attest to the fact that Jesus was the One True God mentioned in the Old Testament. A passage found in Zechariah 11:12, 13 clearly refers to the death of Jesus, but also pertains to His absolute deity. It reads, "And I said unto them, If ye think good, give me my price; and if not, forbear. So they weighed for my price thirty pieces of silver. And the

That Jesus Is God

LORD said unto me, Cast it unto the potter: a goodly price that I was prised at of them. And I took the thirty pieces of silver, and cast them to the potter in the house of the LORD." We can see with eyes of certainty from this passage of scripture that it was the Lord who died on the cross—to be more precise, God manifested in flesh, as a Spirit could not be crucified on a cross.

Before Abraham

A further proof of His absolute deity being demonstrated by events in His earthly ministry is seen in John 8:58, where Jesus said, "Verily, verily, I say unto you, Before Abraham was, I am." He was the great I Am before the birth of Abraham, He was the great I Am during the lifetime of Abraham, He was the great I Am after the death of Abraham, and He remains the great I Am today. As Hebrews 13:8 says, "Jesus Christ, the same yesterday, and to day, and for ever." Hebrews 1:10-12 reminds us: "And, Thou, Lord, in the beginning hast laid the foundation of the earth; and the heavens are the works of thine hands: They shall perish; but thou remainest; and they all shall wax old as doth a garment; And as a vesture shalt thou fold them up, and they shall be changed: but thou art the same, and thy years shall not fail." If we read the entire first chapter of Hebrews, there can be no doubt in our minds as to the fact that the above verses are referring to the Son.

The Way Of The Lord

Returning to the very beginning of the ministry of John the Baptist, we find John being questioned as to just who he is that would give him the right to preach condemnation and repentance in the manner in

All the Fulness

which he is preaching it. From the start, John told them that he was not the Christ. When asked if he were Elias (Elijah), he answered that he was not. Others asked if he were a prophet, and he responded that he was not that either. As they continued to question him, John finally told them that he was, "the voice of one crying in the wilderness" (John 1:23). John continued by saying, "Make straight the way of the Lord, as said the prophet E-sai-as (Isaiah)" (John 1:23). It is quite evident here that John was speaking of Jesus Christ when he uttered these words.

In Isaiah 40:3, we find the scripture that John was referring to when he spoke of Jesus: "The voice of him that crieth in the wilderness, Prepare ye the way of the LORD, make straight in the desert a highway for our God." The evidence is there in plain view for all to see that Isaiah and John were speaking of the same person. The original text of this passage used the word *Jehovah* in place of *Lord*. So, the verse would more accurately read, "Prepare ye the way of Jehovah, make straight in the desert a highway for our God."

Thus, we see that John was the forerunner of the One who was in His absolute deity **Jehovah Our God.** We know from scripture that the One John paved the way for was none other than Jesus Christ Himself. Thus, we have no choice but to admit that Jesus Christ was also Jehovah God. John said in Matthew 3:11, "He that cometh after me is mightier than I." The next verse tells us that Jesus will, ". . .throughly purge his floor, and gather his wheat into the garner." Notice that the scripture states that the floor and the wheat belong to Jesus. The reference to wheat is not a literal one of course, but is an allusion to mankind. Knowing that the Bible refers to man as the son of God in many instances, we

That Jesus Is God

cannot help but see that in saying that we belong to Jesus, we are saying that Jesus is God. For, the Bible itself declares in Matthew 6:24, "No man can serve two masters."

His Temple

Going to Malachi 3:1, we find the following: "BEHOLD, I will send my messenger, and he shall prepare the way before me: and the Lord, whom you seek, shall suddenly come to his temple." In discussing this verse, I take the liberty of quoting A. A. Hodge, a noted and dedicated Trinitarian. In commenting on Malachi 3:1, Hodge says, "This passage self-evidently refers to the Messiah, as it is confirmed by Mark 1:2. The Hebrew term *Adonai*, here translated Lord, is never applied to any other than the Supreme God. The temple, which is sacred to the presence and worship of Jehovah, is called 'His Temple.' "

There are two possible interpretations of the portion of the verse which says, "shall suddenly come to his temple." We will treat the literal interpretation first.

In laying the foundation for Jesus' famous "Temple Cleansing," we go back a few verses, and join Him as He is entering into Jerusalem on the back of a donkey, as the multitude spreads clothing and tree branches in His pathway. Matthew 21:4, 5 tells us that all this was being done so that the prophecy of Zechariah would be fulfilled. In Zechariah 9:9 we find, "Rejoice greatly, O daughter of Zion; shout, O daughter of Jerusalem: behold, thy King cometh unto thee: he is just, and having salvation; lowly, and riding upon an ass, and upon a colt the foal of an ass."

Zechariah 2:10 further confirms that this is the Lord God who is entering into Jerusalem in this manner. It says, "Sing and rejoice, O daughter of Zion: for, lo, I come, and I will dwell in the midst of thee, saith the LORD. Zechariah 14:9 tells us without the least equivocation who this King riding on the back of a donkey really is, when it states, "And the LORD shall be king over all the earth: in that day shall there be one Lord, and his name one." Zechariah 14:5, only makes a solid assertion into an undeniably solid assertion when speaking of the Second Coming of Jesus Christ. It says in part, "And the LORD my God shall come, and all the saints with thee." By comparing this scripture to Acts 1:11, where the angel of the Lord promised the grief stricken disciples that Jesus would return in the manner that He had just left, we are left with no choice but to admit that **Jesus is God.**

The one who entered His temple in Matthew 21, and the One who has promised to return in the same manner in which He left, is God. True to the prophecy of Malachi, Jesus suddenly appeared in His temple. While there, He thoroughly purged it, casting out the money changers and the merchants who were getting rich selling sacrificial doves. In Matthew 21:13 Jesus said, "It is written, My house shall be called the house of prayer; but ye have made it a den of thieves." Just as He suddenly appeared in the temple, He will one day appear for His Bride. And, just as the money changers and dove merchants had no warning, and were caught unprepared, masses of people will have no forewarning, and will not be prepared for His return.

We now approach the symbolical interpretation of the portion of Malachi 3:1 which reads, "shall suddenly come to his temple." This interpretation declares the term *temple* to be in reference to that

That Jesus Is God

fleshly body that Jesus occupied during His brief stay here on earth. The Scriptures say that God suddenly came into His temple. What is more sudden than conception? Conception is a momentary event, and not a progressive one taking a length of time. At one moment there is no life, and the next moment there is life. When the Holy Ghost overshadowed Mary, she conceived in an instantaneous manner, the same as a natural conception. Although the Babe Jesus was not yet born, the body was already the dwelling place of the "Fulness of the Godhead." Thus, God had suddenly come into His temple.

Even the novice Bible student will be quick to admit that the term *temple* is used in the Bible as a synonym for body. Perhaps the best example of this symbolism is found in John 2:19-21, which reads, "Jesus answered and said unto them, Destroy this temple, and in three days I will raise it up. Then said the Jews, Forty and six years was this temple in building, and wilt thou rear it up in three days? But he spake of the temple of his body."

By accepting this interpretation to Malachi, one cannot help but accept the absolute deity of Jesus Christ. But, if you do not choose to accept the symbolic interpretation, and wish to stick to the literal interpretation, then you are still attesting to the absolute deity of Jesus. If the verse is referring to God, then one must admit that Jesus Christ is God, for the action that is prophetically attributed to God is performed by Jesus. If we insist the verse is referring to Jesus, we still must admit that Jesus Christ is God, for Jesus entered a temple referred to as His own, yet built by the Jews unto God. Therefore, if we are to accept the authenticity and the canonicity of Malachi 3:1, we must also accept the Oneness of God.

All the Fulness

The "I Am"

During the earthly sojourn of Jesus, He constantly used the term *I Am* when making reference to Himself. We have already mentioned the instance found in John 8:58, where Jesus candidly stated that,"Before Abraham was, I am." This is but one of several "I Am" scriptures found in the Bible. John 6:35 reads, "I am the bread of life." In John 8:12 Jesus said, "I am the light of the world." Jesus said in John 10:9, "I am the door." Two verses later He said, "I am the good shepherd." But, in Psalm 23:1 we are told that Jehovah (Lord) is the Shepherd. And, in Matthew 19:17 Jesus said that there was none good but God. Therefore, Jesus must be that Good Shepherd, Jehovah.

In John 11:25 Jesus said, "I am the resurrection and the life." Oh, what a statement for Jesus to make—that He is the life. For, in I Timothy 6:16 we find that God alone has immortality. Therefore, in making the statement "I am the resurrection and the life," Jesus is making a personal claim to absolute and eternal deity.

Going further, we find in John 14:6 that Jesus says, "I am the way, the truth, and the life." In John 15:1 He says, "I am the true vine." In John 18 we find the account of the arrest of Jesus by a mob sanctioned by the chief priests and Pharisaical leaders. According to John 18:6, once Jesus told them that "I am he," they retreated and fell to the ground. Evidently the two words "I Am" had such a tremendous effect upon them that they fell to the ground in fear. This is easily understood with the realization that they had come to arrest God manifested in the flesh. When Jesus told them, "I am he," He was doing more than divulging His earthly identity. He was telling them that he was the *I Am*, the one who had existed before Abraham.

In Acts 9 we read of Paul's great conversion, in which he heard a voice from heaven saying, "Saul, Saul, why persecutest thou me?" (Acts 9:4). In the next verse Saul (later Paul) asked the question, "Who art thou, Lord?" In response, the voice says, "I am Jesus whom thou persecutest." From that moment on, Saul turned his back on the life that had been dedicated to the harassment and persecution of Christians, and with the same intensified effort prepared himself for a life and ministry totally committed unto God. Like Moses, Saul had met the great I Am. Once again, when Jesus said, "I Am," He was doing much more than revealing His fleshly identity. He was testifying of His eternal existence.

HIS ABSOLUTE DEITY RELATIVE TO HIS ASCENSION

We now look at the absolute deity of Jesus Christ as shown in His ascension. For reference we once again turn to the Book of Psalms. In Psalm 24:3 we find the word *ascend* used as we read, "Who shall ascend into the hill of the LORD?" Verses 7 through 10 of the same chapter provides us with the prophecy concerning the ascension of Jesus. This portion of scripture which we have referred to previously reads, "Lift up your heads, O ye gates; and be ye lift up, ye everlasting doors; and the King of glory shall come in. Who is the King of glory? The LORD strong and mighty, the LORD mighty in battle. Lift up your heads, O ye gates; even lift them up, ye everlasting doors;

and the King of glory shall come in. Who is this King of glory? The LORD of hosts, he is the King of glory. Se-lah."

The preceding verses reveal the Lord Jesus Christ, the One who ascended, as the King of glory, and as Jehovah of Hosts. But, we are told that He returned from battle, mighty and strong. Can this description be a reference to Jesus Christ? Studying the Word of God, we find that indeed this passage is a prophecy concerning Jesus. Do we not read in Hebrews 2:14, ". . .that through death he might destroy him that had the power of death, that is, the devil." And, in Ephesians 4:8 we read that, "When he ascended up on high, he led captivity captive." This of course, is also referring to Jesus' victory over Satan.

The battle was fought and won at calvary. The last words of Jesus, "It is finished," were the sounds of victory. By them, the veil of the temple was rent in twain, and the way back to God was restored. Paradise, once lost by the disobedience of the first Adam, was now recovered by the total obedience of the second Adam. Who can ever forget the beautiful words spoken by Jesus to the thief on the cross: "Verily, I say unto thee, To day shalt thou be with me in paradise" (Luke 23:43). I am reminded of the hymn which says:

> Death cannot keep his prey—Je-sus my Savior!
> He tore the bars a-way Je-sus my Lord!
> Up from the grave He a-rose, With a might-y triumph o'er His foes;
> He arose a Victor from the dark do-main,
> And He lives for-ev-er with His saints to reign,
> He a-rose! He a-rose! Hal-le-lu-jah! Christ a-rose!

Before He went to the Cross, Jesus could say, "I beheld Satan as lightning fall from heaven" (Luke 10:18). And, in John 12:31, 32, Jesus said, "Now is the judgment of this world: now shall the prince of this world be cast out. And I, if I be lifted up from the earth, will draw all men unto me." Verse 32 has two possible interpretations, and both of them are in harmony with the rest of Scripture. If we interpret the lifting up of Jesus to refer to His ascension, we are on target, as the Word of God plainly teaches that the Holy Spirit could not be sent as a Comforter until Jesus had ascended. If, on the other hand, we interpret the lifting up to pertain to placing Jesus in His rightful position as the Absolute and Eternal Deity, we are once again right on target. For, through the Great Commission we are compelled to go unto all the world, teaching them—yes, teaching them that the fulness of God dwelt in the body of Jesus Christ, and that Jesus paid the eternal price of redemption when He died on the Cross. If we lift up Jesus by our actions and our testimony, all who hear will have the opportunity of receiving eternal salvation.

But, in returning to Psalm 24, a portion quoted earlier, we discover that the One who will return to glory; the One who will ascend triumphantly; and the One to whom the very gates of heaven will open in joyful reception, is none other than Jehovah, the Lord of Hosts. We find that through the actions of Jesus Christ, Jehovah was mighty in battle. Within the confines of Psalm 24, we observe a tremendous proof and an outstanding vindication of the full-orbed deity of Jesus Christ relative to His ascension.

Turning now to Revelation 1:8, we find, "I am Alpha and Omega, the beginning and the ending,

All the Fulness

saith the Lord, which is, and which was, and which is to come, the Almighty." Even the Jehovah's Witnesses assure us that this verse applies to Jehovah, the Lord God Almighty. But, in verses 10 through 13 of the same chapter we find the following: "I was in the Spirit on the Lord's day, and heard behind me a great voice, as of a trumpet, Saying, I am Alpha and Omega, the first and the last: and, What thou seest, write in a book. . .And I turned to see the voice that spake with me. And being turned, I saw seven golden candlesticks; And in the midst of the seven candlesticks one like unto the Son of man. . . ."

So, we discover from these verses that the Almighty Jehovah of verse 8, who is the Alpha and the Omega, is also the Son of Man (Jesus) found in verses 10 through 13. The Great Creator had become our Savior, but had now ascended.

Just in case there remains the least speck of doubt in your mind, we invite your attention to verses 17 and 18 of the same chapter. They reaffirm our position in a most certain manner. We read, "And when I saw him, I fell at his feet as dead. And he laid his right hand upon me, saying unto me. Fear not; I am the first and the last: I am he that liveth, and was dead; and, behold, I am alive for evermore, Amen; and have the keys of hell and of death." So, since there cannot possibly be two *firsts* or two *lasts*, and since there cannot possibly be two *Alphas* or two *Omegas*, we must conclude that Jesus Christ is not only the Son of Man, but the Almighty God and the Everlasting Father as well.

We find in Revelation 2:8 that Jesus said about Himself that He is "the first and the last, which was dead, and is alive." It is interesting to note that five verses later the church in Pergamos is lauded for holding fast the name of Jesus. This refers to a church era in which the doctrine of the trinity was being introduced, along with its heretical triune baptismal formula. It was the Pergamos Church that rejected this triadic introduction, and persisted in true Jesus Name baptism, accompanied by a belief in the absolute deity of Jesus Christ.

In Revelation 4:8 we read of the One who is called "Holy, holy, holy, Lord God Almighty, which was, and is, and is to come." This is in direct correlation with Revelation 1:8. Then in Revelation 4:5 we read of the "seven Spirits of God." Revelation 5:6 tells us that it is Jesus Christ that possesses the seven Spirits of God. Knowing that Revelation is a symbolic book, and being aware that seven is the divine number of completeness and perfection, it would appear that the preceding verses can be explained in relation to the seven Spirits prophetically mentioned by Isaiah. From Isaiah 11:2, in a prophetic reference to Jesus, we find the following, "And the spirit of the LORD shall rest upon him, the spirit of wisdom and understanding, the spirit of counsel and might, the spirit of knowledge and of the fear of the LORD." So, in Jesus Christ, we find the completeness of the Spirit of the Lord. We find in II Corinthians 3:17 that, "The Lord is that Spirit."

Before moving on from this section, there is one further scripture I wish to present. The passage does not concern the ascension of Jesus, but rather the appearance of the New Jerusalem as it comes down from God out of heaven. The beginning of this section referred to the Alpha and Omega, and showed that Jesus Christ is the Alpha and Omega, the

Beginning and the Ending, the First and the Last, and the Author and Finisher of our faith (Revelation 1:8, 11).

Reading from Revelation 21:6, 7 we find the following: "And he said unto me, It is done. I am Alpha and Omega, the beginning and the end (Compare with Hebrews 7:3). I will give unto him that is athirst of the fountain of the water of life freely (Compare with John 7:37, 38). He that overcometh shall inherit all things; and I will be his God, and he shall be my son." Thus, we find the risen, exalted, returning Lord claiming that He is our God, and that we are His sons.

HIS ABSOLUTE DEITY RELATIVE TO HIS RETURN

Of all the proofs pertaining to the absolute deity of Jesus, those relating to His return are the most convincing and intriguing. In this particular area of our study we first turn our attention to the Book of Job. In Chapter 19, verses 23-27, we read a most lucid, prophetic statement uttered by Job at a time when he was being sorely tried. His profound pronouncement reads, "Oh that my words were now written! oh that they were printed in a book! That they were graven with an iron pen and lead in the rock for ever! For I know that my redeemer liveth, and that he shall stand at the latter day upon the earth: And though after my skin worms destroy this body, yet in my flesh shall I see God: Whom I shall see for myself, and mine eyes shall behold, and not another; though my reins be consumed within me."

That Jesus Is God

There are several items mentioned in these inspired verses that warrant our special attention. First, Job made it absolutely clear that the statement he was about to make was a profound one—one of utmost importance. Next, Job said that the One he was referring to was his Redeemer. Job then goes on to tell us that his Redeemer will stand upon the earth at the latter day. Finally, Job informs us that in his glorified body he will see his Redeemer. Jehovah-God was the Redeemer of the Old Testament, while Jesus is the Redeemer of the New Testament.

When we remember that Job's statement was made early in the Old Testament era, we become aware of its amazing profundity. Is it any wonder that Job prefaced the statement in the manner in which he did?

Turning to Zechariah 14:3-5, we witness a further confirmation of the words of Job: "Then shall the LORD go forth, and fight against those nations, as when he fought in the day of battle. And his feet shall stand in that day upon the mount of Olives, which is before Jerusalem on the east, and the mount of Olives shall cleave in the midst thereof toward the east and toward the west...and the LORD my God shall come, and all the saints with thee."

In the aforementioned verses found in Zechariah, we find complete agreement with those from the Book of Job. Chapters 12 and 14 of Zechariah are often referred to as the *Armageddon Chapters*, as they speak of events immediately preceding and precipitating the return of Jesus Christ to earth to set up His millennial kingdom. As does Job, these two chapters also speak of the return of the Lord. The two words "shall stand," found in both books, are of

All the Fulness

outstanding consequence. Job says, "He shall stand at the latter day upon the earth" (Job 19:25). And, Zechariah declares, "And his feet shall stand in that day upon the mount of Olives" (Zechariah 14:4). Both of these passages plainly declare that He who will stand upon the Mount of Olives in the last days is none other than Jehovah my God (Zechariah) and (Job).

If we are to maintain a belief in the verity of God's Word, then we of necessity must accept the prophetic utterances of both Job and Zechariah. They were not mistaken when they foretold of the return of Jehovah-God to the Mount of Olives. They were in no way contradicting the mass of scripture which prophesies that Jesus Christ will be the one who returns to the Mount of Olives. Just as God, in the form of Jesus Christ came to redeem mankind, He will once again return to earth in the form of Jesus Christ. "For in him dwelleth all the fulness of the Godhead bodily"(Colossians 2:9). We repeat, Jesus Christ is **all** of God, not just one-third of Him.

Turning to a well-know passage of scripture found in Acts 1:9-12, we discover that indeed it is Jesus Christ who is returning to the Mount of Olives. It reads, "And when he had spoken these things, while they beheld, he was taken up; and a cloud received him out of their sight. And while they looked steadfastly toward heaven as he went up, behold, two men stood by them in white apparel; Which also said, Ye men of Galilee, why stand ye gazing up into heaven? this same Jesus, which is taken up from you into heaven, shall so come in like manner as ye have seen him go into heaven. Then returned they unto Jerusalem from the mount called

Olivet, which is from Jerusalem a sabbath day's journey."

He who departed from this earth at Olivet, is returning to the mount from which He left. Zechariah 14 and Acts 1 will both be fulfilled by one act, performed by only one Man—Jesus Christ; the Absolute and Eternal Deity; the Alpha and Omega; the only God mankind will ever know; the only Supreme Deity that has or ever will exist.

In Daniel 7:9 we read an arresting statement which says, "I beheld till the thrones were cast down, and the Ancient of days did sit, whose garment was white as snow, and the hair of his head like the pure wool: his throne was like the fiery flame, and his wheels as burning fire." Compare this to what we read in Revelation 1:13-15: "And in the midst of the seven candlesticks one like unto the Son of man, clothed with a garment down to the foot, and girt about the paps with a golden girdle. His head and his hairs were white like wool, as white as snow; and his eyes were as a flame of fire; And his feet like unto fine brass, as if they burned in a furnace; and his voice as the sound of many waters."

Returning to Daniel 7, we find the following: "I saw in the night visions, and behold, one like the Son of man came with the clouds of heaven, and came to the Ancient of days, and they brought him near before him" (Daniel 7:13). However, when we read verse 22 of Daniel 7, we discover that the One who is returning is *The Ancient of Days*. The verse reads, "Until the Ancient of days came, and judgment was given to the saints of the most High." So, He who is returning is not only the Son of Man (Jesus), but He is also the Ancient of Days (Jehovah-God).

All the Fulness

In the afore-mentioned verses we see displayed both the perfect humanity and the absolute divinity of Jesus Christ. He is the Son of Man as to His humanity, and the Ancient of Days as to His deity. Daniel's presentation of the humanity and divinity of our Lord is quite similar to that introduced in Isaiah 9:6; "For unto us a child is born, unto us a son is given: and the government shall be upon his shoulder: and his name shall be called Wonderful, Counsellor, The mighty God, The everlasting Father, The Prince of Peace." Therefore, we find that the Son is also the *Everlasting Father* (Isaiah 9:6), and the *Ancient of Days* (Daniel 7:22). Micah 5:2, in speaking of Jesus, says, "whose goings forth have been from of old, from everlasting." Hebrews 13:8 says, "Jesus Christ the same yesterday, and to day, and for ever."

Understanding these scriptures helps us to better comprehend the words of Jesus as He was hanging on the Cross. When He cried out, "My God, my God, why hast thou forsaken me," it was simply His perfect humanity crying out to His deity. In a sense, His deity had temporarily forsaken His humanity so that He could be the sin-bearer and that perfect sacrifice (Leviticus 16:22; Habakkuk 1:13; and II Corinthians 5:21). The passages found in Daniel and Isaiah also help us to visualize Jesus as the Lamb standing before the throne, while at the same time being God sitting upon the throne (Revelation 5:6, 7). He who is returning is the Ancient of Days. The child that was born was also the Mighty God.

Focusing our attention now on the New Testament, we find that the Apostle Paul states in his letter to Titus that He who is returning is none other than the Great God. Titus 2:13 reads, "Looking for that

That Jesus Is God

blessed hope, and the glorious appearing of the great God and our Saviour Jesus Christ." Notice the words used by the inspired writer in this verse: "the glorious appearing of the great God." Doesn't this sound like the One Job was looking for? Job said that this returning One would be his God and his redeemer, and that His feet would be planted upon the earth in those latter days. "In my flesh shall I see God: Whom I shall see for myself, and my eyes shall behold, and not another" (Job 19:26, 27).

Paul further states in I Timothy 6:14-16; ". . .until the appearing of our Lord Jesus Christ: Which in his times he shall shew, who is the blessed and only Potentate, the King of kings, and the Lord of lords; Who only hath immortality. . . ." From Revelation 19:16 we see that Jesus Christ is the King of Kings and the Lord of Lords. So, at His appearing, Jesus shall show beyond a shadow of a doubt that in addition to being the Redeemer; He is the King of Kings; the Lord of Lords; the Blessed and Only Potentate; and God Over All, Blessed For Ever.

Going one step further, we find the following in Revelation 22:6, 7: "The Lord God of the holy prophets sent his angel to shew unto his servants the things which must shortly be done. Behold, I come quickly." Notice here that it is the Lord God (Jehovah) who is coming again. However, in verse 16 of the same chapter we read, "I Jesus have sent mine angel." By now, it should be quite clear that **one** angel is being sent by **one** Deity, and that His name is Jesus. He is the Son of Man, while at the same time He is the Lord God.

We receive further confirmation for our contention from verses 12 and 13 of Revelation 22, which say in part, "And, behold, I come quickly; and my reward is with me. . .I am Alpha and Omega, the beginning and the end, the first and the last." Some, such as the Jehovah's Witnesses, who deny the deity of Jesus Christ, deny that Jesus is the Alpha and Omega of Revelation 1:8. But, the verses found in Revelation 22 fully consolidate the belief that He who was the Son born in Bethlehem, later became the Redeemer, and will some day return, is none other than the Alpha and the Omega, the Almighty, and the Lord God of the holy prophets.

In Revelation 22:7 God says, "Behold I come quickly." In Revelation 22:20 Jesus says, "Surely I come quickly." John, the writer of Revelation adds, "Even so, come, Lord Jesus."

COMPARATIVE PROOFS OF THE ABSOLUTE DEITY OF JESUS CHRIST

There is basically only one pattern of study regarding the Oneness of the Godhead—to show that qualities and actions attributed to one manifestation are also attributed to the others. When making such a comparison, we must be careful to use only exclusive attributes. For example, it would be feasible for three persons in the Godhead to be powerful, but only one can be **all-powerful**. By showing that both the Father and the Son are said to be all-powerful, we are showing that They are one in the same. This has been the format of this chapter, as well as the book itself. We refer to this system of presentation as Comparative Proofs. Before ending this chapter, I wish to present some additional comparative proofs to the absolute deity of Jesus Christ.

The Shepherd

In the Old Testament, Psalm 23, God revealed Himself as *Jehovah-Roi* (Jehovah my Shepherd). Psalm 23:1 reads, "The LORD is my shepherd; I shall not want." The same thought is expressed in Isaiah 40:10, 11 where we read, "Behold, the LORD GOD will come with a strong hand, and his arm shall rule for him: behold, his reward is with him, and his work before him. He shall feed his flock like a shepherd: he shall gather the lambs with his arm, and carry them in his bosom, and shall gently lead those that are with young."

From Isaiah 53:1, 2 we learn that Jesus is the *Arm of the Lord* referred to in Isaiah 40:10. This in turn gives us a better understanding of the term "Right Hand of God," which simply means the power or the authority of God. In Isaiah 40:10, we are told that the Lord God is returning with His reward. However, we find in Revelation 22:12 that Jesus is returning with His reward. Are two returning, each bearing His own reward? We think not. If we remain open-minded and allow our pre-conceived prejudices to fall by the wayside, we cannot help but admit that there is but one Shepherd, and that mankind will experience just one returning Deity bringing His reward. Isaiah and John wrote of the same "person."

John 10:11 quotes Jesus as saying, "I am the good shepherd." Hebrews 13:20 refers to Jesus as "that great shepherd of the sheep." I Peter 5:4 speaks of Jesus as the "chief Shepherd." Surely, there can be no greater shepherd than the Chief Shepherd. Yet, the

All the Fulness

Lord God is referred to as the Shepherd. If Jesus and God are not the same, then Jesus is greater than God. So, we must conclude that Jehovah, the Shepherd of Psalm 23, has revealed Himself in Jesus, the Shepherd of the New Testament.

The Rock

In various places in the Old Testament God revealed Himself unto Israel as their Rock. Psalm 18:2 reads, "The LORD is my rock." Psalm 42:9 says, "I will say unto God my rock, Why hast thou forgotten me?" In Psalm 62:2 we find, "He only is my rock and my salvation." We find the following in Psalm 78:35: "And they remembered that God was their rock." Going to Psalm 89:26 we read, "Thou art my father, my God, and the rock of my salvation." And, in reading Psalm 94:22, we find the psalmist saying, "God is the rock of my refuge."

Leaving Psalms, we find in Deuteronomy 32:4, "He is the Rock, his work is perfect. Verse 15 of the same chapter reads, "Then he forsook God which made him, and lightly esteemed the Rock of his salvation." And in verse 31 of the same chapter we find the following: "For their rock is not as our Rock." In I Samuel 2:2 we see, "Neither is there any rock like our God." II Samuel 22:32 asks the questions, "For who is God, save the LORD? and who is a rock, save our God?" Verse 47 of the same chapter states, "The LORD liveth; and blessed be my rock; and exalted be the God of the rock of my salvation." Finally, in Isaiah 17:10 we find, "Because thou hast forgotten the God of thy salvation, and hast not been mindful of the rock of thy strength. . . ."

From the numerous scriptures we have just

That Jesus Is God

quoted, it is most obvious that God is **That Rock.** And, everything is brought into perfect perspective by one short statement made in I Corinthians 10:4— "And that Rock was Christ."

The Rock, Jesus Christ, found in the New Testament, who is the Chief Cornerstone, and is the Stone rejected by the builders, is none other than the Rock, Jehovah-God, of the Old Testament.

The First And The Last

Although this subject was treated in an earlier section of the chapter, it is felt that it warrants further treatment here. Reading from Isaiah 44:6 we find, "Thus saith the LORD the King of Israel, and his redeemer the LORD of hosts; I am the first, and I am the last; and beside me there is no God. It is clearly indicated here, and common sense tells us, that there cannot be two *first* and two *lasts*. Verse 8 of this same chapter further reinforces this thought when it asks the question, "Is there a God beside me?" and gives the answer, "There is no God, I know not any."

Isaiah 48:12 says, "Hearken unto me, O Jacob and Israel, my called; I am he; I am the first, I also am the last." The First and the Last is the Great I Am. In Isaiah 41:4 we find," I the LORD, the first, and with the last; I am he." In Isaiah 43:10, 11 we see, "I am he: before me there was no God formed, neither shall there be after me. I, even I, am the LORD; and beside me there is no saviour."

The preceding scriptures are cyrstal clear. There is only one First and Last. For more than one to exist would be indeed incomprehensible. He who is the Creator, is the Redeemer and Savior also.

Turning now to the New Testament we find

words like these: "I am the first and the last: I am he that liveth, and was dead; and, behold, I am alive for evermore, Amen; and have the keys of hell and death" (Revelation 1:17, 18). Verse 11 of the same chapter also states that Jesus is the "Alpha and Omega, the first and the last." Then in Revelation 2:8 we read in reference to Jesus, "These things saith the first and the last, which was dead, and is alive." Since we have already established that there can only be one first and one last, the scripture must be referring to God the Father. And, since the scripture says that He was dead, but is now alive, it of necessity must be referring to Jesus the Son, for God the Father never died. Therefore, we are once more left with no choice but to admit that Jesus Christ and God the Father are **ONE!**

Finally, we read the words of the Returning Christ in Revelation 22:13: "I am Alpha and Omega, the beginning and the end, the first and the last." Yes, He is Jehovah in the Old Testament and Jesus Christ in the New Testament.

The King

We now look at the fourth Comparative Proof—The King. In the Old Testament Jehovah was the King of His people Israel. We remember well the episode of I Samuel 8 where the elders of Israel asked Samuel for a king so that they might be as the other nations of the world. It was never God's intention for them to have a monarchical form of government, as He fully intended for them to remain a theocracy. However, He did submit to their wishes and allow Samuel to anoint a king over Israel.

In I Samuel 8:7, we find the following: "And the

That Jesus Is God

LORD said unto Samuel, Hearken unto the voice of the people in all that they say unto thee: for they have not rejected thee, but they have rejected me, that I should not reign over them." Jehovah was their king. He was their supreme ruler. This fact is substantiated in numerous Old Testament scriptures, a few of which we will now quote. I Samuel 12:12 says, "...when the LORD your GOD was your king." Psalm 10:16 reads, "The LORD is King for ever and ever." We find in Psalm 29:10, "The LORD sitteth King for ever." And, in Psalm 44:4 we see the following: "Thou art my King, O God."

Isaiah 6:5 says, "For mine eyes have seen the King, the LORD of hosts." Going forward to Isaiah 32:1, we read, "BEHOLD, a king shall reign in righteousness." Verses 17 and 22 of Isaiah 33 tell us who the King is. We find, "Thine eyes shall see the king in his beauty: they shall behold the land that is very far off. For the LORD is our judge, the LORD is our lawgiver, the LORD is our king; he will save us." Finally, Isaiah 41:21 refers to Him as the "King of Jacob," while Isaiah 44:6 calls Him the "King of Israel."

In Jeremiah 10:7 we find God referred to as, "King of nations." Verse 10 of the same chapter calls Him, "an everlasting king." However, Jeremiah 23:5, in speaking prophetically of Jesus Christ, says, "Behold, the days come, saith the LORD, that I will raise unto David a righteous Branch, and a King shall reign and prosper, and shall execute judgment and justice in the earth." The next verse tells us the name He will be called: "his name whereby he shall be called, THE LORD OUR RIGHTEOUSNESS." In Daniel 4:37, we find that Nebuchadnezzar referred to God as "the

King of heaven." Then in Zechariah 14:9, we have the beautiful verse which reads, "And the LORD shall be king over all the earth: in that day shall there be one LORD, and his name one." Our final scripture found in the Old Testament, Malachi 1:14, reads, "I am a great King, saith the LORD of hosts."

We now turn to the New Testament where the true identity of the King is divulged. In John 1:49, Nathanael, in his first meeting with Jesus, said, "Thou art the Son of God; thou art the King of Israel." But, in going back to Isaiah 44:6, we find that these very words were used in making reference to God. In Matthew 5:35 Jesus personally referred to the city of Jerusalem as, "the city of the great King." Who then was the King of Jerusalem? In Hebrews 7:2 Melchisedec is referred to as "King of righteousness" and "King of Sa-lem" (Jerusalem). Hebrews 6:20 informs us that Jesus was "an high priest for ever after the order of Mel-chis-ed-ec." So, if this order of priesthood included the kingship of Jerusalem, then Jesus, like Melchisedec was the King of Jerusalem.

We go now to John 12:12-15 where we find the account of Jesus' triumphant entry into Jerusalem. "On the next day much people that were come to the feast, when they heard that Jesus was coming to Jerusalem, Took branches of palm trees, and went forth to meet him, and cried, Hosanna: Blessed is the King of Israel that cometh in the name of the Lord. And Jesus, when he had found a young ass, sat thereon; as it is written, Fear not, daughter of Sion: behold, thy King cometh, sitting on an ass's colt. He, of whom it was said in John 1:29, "Behold the Lamb of God," it could have been said, "Behold the King."

In John 19:14 we find Pontius Pilate referring to

That Jesus Is God

Jesus in the following manner: "Behold your King!" And in Matthew 27:37, we find that the words "THIS IS JESUS THE KING OF THE JEWS" were written above the head of Christ as He hung on the Cross. This epitaph was written on the orders of Pilate himself. I Timothy 6:15 refers to Jesus as, "only Potentate, the King of kings, and the Lord of lords." In Revelation 15:3 Jesus is referred to as, "thou King of saints." Revelation 17:14 and 19:16 speak of Jesus as "KING OF KINGS, AND LORD OF LORDS."

Once again we are faced with making a decision—the two options are adherence to God's Word, or belief in a doctrine concocted in the minds of man. A Kingdom can have but one king. There can be but **one** "King of Israel," "King of Nations," "King of Saints," or "King of Glory." Those who will attempt to dispute this fact display a lack of knowledge concerning the monarchical system of government. Israel does not recognize it, but the *Conquering King* they are awaiting visited them almost 2000 years ago in the form of a *Suffering Messiah*. For those still possessing the least bit of doubt, we invite you to look up every New Testament reference to the Heavenly King. You will discover, that without exception, they refer to the Lord Jesus Christ. There just cannot possibly be two King of Kings or two Lord of Lords.

The Redeemer And Savior

In the fifth Comparative Proof we discuss the attributes of Redeemer and Savior. Following our now established pattern of study, we begin with scripture from the Old Testament. Job says, "For I know that my redeemer liveth, and that he shall stand at the

All the Fulness

latter day upon the earth: And though after my skin worms destroy this body, yet in my flesh shall I see God" (Job 19:25, 26). Four points are worth noting in this passage: (1) Job knew his redeemer, (2) He knew that He was alive, (3) He knew that He was God, and (4) He knew that in the latter day his redeemer would return to earth. These four points are worth remembering.

Psalm 19:14 reads, "Let the words of my mouth, and the meditation of my heart, be acceptable in thy sight, O LORD, my strength, and my Redeemer." In Proverbs 23:11 we find, "For their redeemer is mighty; he shall plead their cause with thee." The words of the prophet in Isaiah 41:14 are, "I will help thee, saith the LORD, and thy redeemer, the Holy One of Israel." Then, as we turn farther into the pages of Isaiah, we find the following: "As for our redeemer, the LORD of hosts is his name, the Holy One of Israel" (Isaiah 47:4).

From the preceding scriptures and others found in the Old Testament, it is quite clear that Jehovah was the Redeemer of His people in the Old Testament. However, the meaning of the word *redeemer* is "To set free by the paying of a ransom; to deliver from sin and its penalities, as by a sacrifice made for the sinner; or to fulfill a promise or a pledge" (Webster's New World Dictionary). The Hebrew word used is *Gaal*. From the above description the term Redeemer can be referring to none other than Jesus Christ. If God the Father had sent His Son Jesus down to die for the sins of the world, could He possibly qualify as a Redeemer? Yet, the Old Testament refers to God as the Redeemer in numerous places. Throughout the Old Testament God promised His people that one day He would buy them back. He kept His promise when Jesus Christ gave His life on Calvary. God did not send His son—He veiled Himself in a fleshly body and came **PERSONALLY.**

The same thought is presented in Isaiah 49:26, in which we read, "And all flesh shall know that I the LORD am thy Saviour and thy Redeemer, the mighty One of Jacob." And in Isaiah 59:20 we read, "And the Redeemer shall come to Zion, and unto them that turn from transgression in Jacob, saith the LORD." This continuity of thought is maintained in Isaiah 60:16 where we read, "I the LORD am thy Saviour and thy Redeemer, the mighty One of Jacob." And finally, we find in Isaiah 63:16, "thou, O LORD, art our father, our redeemer; thy name is from everlasting."

Who is the Everlasting Father who became our Redeemer? The answer is found in Isaiah 9:6, and is confirmed by numerous New Testament scriptures. It reads, "For unto us a child is born, unto us a son is given: and the government shall be upon his shoulder: and his name shall be called Wonderful, Counsellor, The mighty God, the Everlasting Father, The Prince of Peace."

The New Testament leaves us without a shadow of doubt concerning the identity of the Redeemer and Savior. What can be more plain than the words of Matthew 1:21 which say, "And she shall bring forth a son, and thou shalt call his name JESUS: for he shall save his people from their sins." Verse 23 of the same chapter tells us that He shall be Emmanuel, which being interpreted is, *God with us.* When we link this verse with Luke 1:68 which says, "Blessed be the Lord God of Israel; for he hath visited and redeemed his people," we again discover that when Jesus was born in Bethlehem, God indeed visited His people Israel.

God became flesh for the redemptive purpose. The Child born, the Son given, the Mighty God, and the Everlasting Father visited earth veiled in the flesh of one human body. For thirty-three and one half years the Almighty God lived in that fleshly temple so that He might become that pure and undefiled Redemptive Lamb. Genesis 22:8 reads, "God will provide himself a lamb." Just as God provided the sacrificial lamb for Abraham on Mount Moriah, He provided it on Calvary. This time, however, the lamb was Himself. I Peter 2:24 says, "Who his own self bare our sins in his own body on the tree." The Great Creator had become our Savior—not His Son.

The New Testament is filled with scriptures which point to the fact that Jesus Christ is the Redeemer of mankind. Therefore, we must conclude that Jehovah, the Redeemer of the Old Testament, revealed Himself and visited His people for the redemptive purpose in the New Testament. His name is Jesus!

The Creator

The sixth Comparative proof concerns the identity of the Creator as shown by both Old Testament and New Testament scripture. There is much scripture in the Old Testament attesting to the fact that God was the Creator. However, when we go over into the New Testament we find these accomplishments attributed to Jesus.

In Genesis 1:1 we read, "In the beginning God created the heaven and the earth." Quickly going to the New Testament, we read an almost identical account in John 1:1, 3: "In the beginning was the

That Jesus Is God

Word, and the Word was with God, and the Word was God. All things were made by him; and without him was not anything made that was made." There is certainly no room for error or misinterpretation when reading the foregoing scriptures. God was the Creator of ALL.

Reading from Job 33:4 we find, "The Spirit of God hath made me, and the breath of the Almighty hath given me life." Then in Psalm 33:6 we read, "By the word of the LORD were the heavens made; and all the host of them by the breath of his mouth." This concurs with Psalm 104:30 which says, "Thou sendest forth thy spirit, they are created: and thou renewest the face of the earth."

Turning to Isaiah 40:28 we read, "Hast thou not known? hast thou not heard, that the everlasting God, the LORD, the Creator of the ends of the earth, fainteth not, neither is weary? there is no searching of his understanding." In Isaiah 44:24 God is referred to as both Creator and Redeemer. The verse reads as follows: "Thus saith the LORD, thy redeemer, and he that formed thee from the womb, I am the LORD that maketh all things; that stretcheth forth the heavens alone; that spreadeth abroad the earth by myself." So, not only does this verse clearly show us that God is both Creator and Redeemer, but it also states that God handled all creation **ALONE.** In other words, when He said in Genesis 1:26, "Let us make man in our image," He was not chairing a three-man Creation Committee.

To further strengthen our point, we go to Malachi 2:10, where we find the following: "Have we not all one father? hath not one God created us?" This links with Ephesians 4:6 in the New Testament which categorically states: "One God and Father of all, who is above all, and through all, and in you all."

We observed in John 1:1, 3 that *God the Creator* was the Word. Skipping down to verse 14 of the same chapter, we find that "the Word was made flesh, and dwelt among us." What can this possibly mean other than God dwelt in His fulness in the body of the man Christ Jesus? I Corinthians 8:6 further substantiates this fact in saying, "But to us there is but one God, the Father, of whom are all things, and we in him; and one Lord Jesus Christ, by whom are all things, and we by him."

Colossians 1:16, 17, in making reference to Jesus, says, "For by him were all things created, that are in heaven. . .all things were created by him, and for him: And he is before all things, and by him all things consist." Jehovah-Jesus is both Creator and Redeemer. The Word of God teaches it no other way.

The Light

"God is light, and in him is no darkness at all" (I John 1:5). With this verse we introduce our seventh and final Comparative Proof—the Attribute of being *The Light.* Psalm 27:1 makes this statement: "The LORD is my light and my salvation." Isaiah 60:19 tells us, "The sun shall be no more thy light by day; neither for brightness shall the moon give light unto thee: but the LORD shall be unto thee an everlasting light, and thy God thy glory." There is also a portion of a verse tucked away in Micah 7:8 which says, "When I sit in darkness, the LORD shall be a light unto me." Habakkuk 3:3, 4 declares, "God came from Te-man, and the Holy One from mount Par-an. Se-lah. His glory covered the heavens, and the earth was full of his praise. And his brightness was as the light."

That Jesus Is God

We discovered earlier from I Timothy 6:15, 16 that Jesus Christ is, "...the blessed and only Potentate, the King of kings, and Lord of lords; Who only hath immortality, dwelling in the light which no man can approach unto...." When Simeon looked upon the infant Jesus in the temple, he said, "A light to lighten the Gentiles, and the glory of thy people Israel" (Luke 2:32). In the Gospel of John Jesus is referred to as "that Light" (John 1:8) and "the true Light" (John 1:9). In John 8:12 Jesus unequivocally stated, "I am the light of the world." In John 9:5 He repeats this assertion by saying, "As long as I am in the world, I am the light of the world." And in John 12:35 we read, "Then Jesus said unto them, Yet a little while is the light with you." There should be no doubt in the mind of the reader as to the fact that Jesus was referring to Himself in this instance.

To a certain extent every true Christian is a light. The degree to which we are a light is directly proportional to the degree that we are Christ-like. The more Christ-like we become, the more we allow His Spirit to emanate from our very being. As Paul said, we allow our Christ-like nature to increase at the expense of our personal or carnal nature. In Matthew 5:14 Jesus Said, "Ye are the light of the world." In Acts 13:47 Paul states that Jesus called him to be, "a light of the Gentiles." Paul, in writing to the Ephesians, said, "For ye were sometimes darkness, but now are ye light in the Lord" (Ephesians 5:8).

CONCLUSION

In concluding this rather lengthy, yet most significant chapter, "That Jesus Is God," we are confident that sincere readers have obtained a true picture of the relationship between Jesus Christ of the New Testament and Jehovah of the Old Testament. The evidence presented is irrefutable in that it came directly from the Word of God. We are well aware that by taking a few selected scriptures out of context, almost any doctrine can be presented. But, the myriad of scriptural references introduced in this chapter attest to the validity of the assertions made. For centuries the *Truth* was buried under the rubbish heap of heresy and tradition. We thank God that in these last days we are witnessing a return to the True Apostolic Doctrine.

3

THAT JESUS IS THE SON

Some may feel, when reading the title of this chapter, that it is an unnecessary one. Their feelings would be based on the stark reality that all Christendom believes that "Jesus is the Son." "No Christian denomination has ever denied that Jesus is the Son of God," we hear them say. We could not agree with them more. However, the purpose of this chapter is to present the Sonship of Jesus as it is presented in the Word of God, as opposed to the manner in which traditional theologians have taught it over the past several centuries. In this chapter we will show that the Sonship of Jesus is not eternal.

Two scriptures which vividly point out that His Sonship was not "from eternity to eternity" are Hebrews 1:5 and I Corinthians 15:27, 28. In Hebrews 1:5 we read, "For unto which of the angels said he at any time, Thou art my Son, this day have I begotten thee?" And in I Corinthians 15:27, 28 we find the following: "For he hath put all things under his feet. But when he saith all things are put under him, it is

All the Fulness

manifest that he is excepted, which did put all things under him. And when all things shall be subdued unto him, then shall the Son also himself be subject unto him that put all things under him, that God may be all in all." We shall refer to these verses later in the chapter, but for the moment let us view the Sonship simply as it is presented in the Bible.

Return with me to Isaiah 9:6, where we once more read, "For unto us a child is born, unto us a son is given." Going back to Isaiah 7:14, we find, "Therefore the LORD himself shall give you a sign; Behold a virgin shall conceive, and bear a son, and shall call his name Immanuel." And Micah 5:2 says, "But thou, Beth-lehem Eph-ra-tah, though thou be little among the thousands of Judah, yet out of thee shall he come forth unto me that is to be ruler in Israel; whose goings forth have been from of old, from everlasting."

All the preceding scriptures clearly show that the Sonship of Jesus had a definite beginning. Contrary to trinitarian tenets, the eternal deity of Jesus is not dependent upon His deity, but by no stretch of the imagination was His deity dependent upon His Sonship.

MATTHEW 1

Matthew 1:18-23 reads in the following manner: "Now the birth of Jesus Christ was on this wise: When as his mother Mary was espoused to Joseph, before they came together, she was found with child of the Holy Ghost. Then Joseph her husband, being a just man, and not willing to make her a publick example, was minded to put her away privily. But while he thought on these things, behold, the angel of the Lord appeared unto him in a dream, saying, Joseph, thou son of David, fear not to take unto thee Mary thy wife: for that which is conceived in her is of the Holy Ghost. And she shall bring forth a son, and thou shalt call his name JESUS: for he shall save his people from their sins. Now all this was done, that it might be fulfilled which was spoken of the Lord by the prophet, saying, Behold, a virgin shall be with child, and shall bring forth a son, and they shall call his name Emmanuel, which being interpreted is, God with us."

In these verses we discover that a very special human body was to be formed in the womb of Mary. Though still a virgin, Mary would become the mother of a baby boy. Although the unborn child would go through a normal development, and the eventual birth would be no different than that of other infants, the conception was anything but ordinary. For, we are told that, "That which is conceived in her is of the Holy Ghost" (Matthew 1:20).

LUKE 1

Luke's account of the Annunciation reads, "And in the sixth month the angel Gabriel was sent from God unto a city of Galilee, named Nazareth, To a virgin espoused to a man whose name was Joseph, of the house of David; and the virgin's name was Mary. And the angel came in unto her, and said, Hail, thou that art highly favoured, the Lord is with thee: blessed art thou among women. And when she saw him, she was troubled at his saying, and cast in her mind what manner of salutation this should be. And the angel said unto her, Fear not, Mary: for thou hast found favour with God. And, behold, thou shalt conceive in thy womb, and bring forth a son, and shalt call his name JESUS. He shall be great, and shall be called the Son of the Highest: and the Lord God shall give unto him the throne of his father David: And he shall reign over the house of Jacob for ever; and of his kingdom there shall be no end. Then said Mary unto the angel; How shall this be, seeing I know not a man? And the angel answered and said unto her, The Holy Ghost shall come upon thee, and the power of the Highest shall overshadow thee: therefore also that holy thing which shall be born of thee shall be called the Son of God" (Luke 1:26-35).

We see from these scriptures that both Mary and her future husband Joseph were told of the event that was about to take place. The Bible informs us that the Angel of the Lord informed Mary of what was to happen just prior to the conception. Joseph was told sometime later—perhaps after it became apparent that his bride-to-be was pregnant. The angel was foretelling of a soon-coming Sonship, not one that had existed from eternity.

HE WAS MADE

Matthew 1 traces the lineage of Joseph, the man who assumed the role of earthly father to Jesus, back to the patriarch David. Various New Testament scriptures point to the fact that Mary, the mother of Jesus, was also of the Davidic line. Thus, Jesus was the answer to a prophetic promise made concerning the throne.

But, let us not forget the words spoken to Mary

That Jesus Is the Son

by the angel: "Therefore also that holy thing which shall be born of thee shall be called the Son of God" (Luke 1:35). Jesus was the Son of Man because He was born of Mary, but at the same time He was the Son of God because He was conceived of the Holy Ghost. He became a son for the purpose of redemption. Hebrews 2:9 sets forth this premise in crystal clear language: "But we see Jesus, who was made a little lower than the angels for the suffering of death...that he by the grace of God should taste death for every man." This position is further stated in verse 14 of the same chapter, where we find, "Forasmuch then as the children are partakers of flesh and blood, he also himself likewise took part of the same; that through death he might destroy him that had the power of death, that is, the devil."

Hebrews 2:16, 17 further confirms the redemptive purpose of the Sonship of Jesus: "For verily he took not on him the nature of angels; but he took on him the seed of Abraham. Wherefore in all things it behoved him to be made like unto his brethren, that he might be a merciful and faithful high priest in things pertaining to God, to make reconciliation for the sins of the people." The writer of Hebrews is telling us that upon His birth, Jesus did not become a spiritual being, but a human. He became flesh and blood—a man that through complete obedience could become that perfect sacrifice for the redemption of fallen man. Through the shedding of His human blood, the sacrifice for all of mankind would be paid. He became a Son in order to redeem us from the inherent sinful state caused by the fall of our father Adam.

Notice how the word *"made"* is used in scripture in connection with the Sonship of our Lord Jesus

All the Fulness

Christ. Galatians 4:4 tells us that, "When the fulness of the time was come, God sent forth his Son, made of a woman, made under the law." And repeating Hebrews 2:17, we find, "Wherefore in all things it behoved him to be made like unto his brethren." In Philippians 2:7, 8 we find the following: "But made himself of no reputation, and took upon him the form of a servant, and was made in the likeness of men: And being found in fashion as a man, he humbled himself, and became obedient unto death, even the death of the cross." *The Moffatt Translation* of verse 8 reads, "And appearing in human form, he humbly stooped in his obedience even to his obedience even to die, and to die upon the cross."

The Sonship had a definite beginning and purpose. Those espousing the trinity do not appear to have a role for the Son other than that of being redeemer. Thus, throughout the remainder of eternity He fills the inactive position of the eternal second person in the Godhead. Regardless of one's concept of the Godhead, there is but one active and meaningful role for the Sonship to play—that of the Redeemer of mankind. If we are to insist on maintaining a belief in the triplicity of gods, then we are forced to relegate Jesus Christ to a secondary, inactive, "figurehead" role in the Godhead. For, we find that prior to His birth God himself took care of all matters. And, shortly after Jesus' death the Holy Spirit took over. So, after Jesus had fulfilled the role of Redeemer, His job was complete, and there was nothing left for Him to do. Had it not been for the redemptive role of JESUS Christ, mankind would never have known Him as the Son. The Scripture plainly teaches us that God himself became the Son for the redemption of *Fallen Man*.

That Jesus Is the Son

HIS LIMITED HUMANITY

Gordon Magee, in his book *Is Jesus In The Godhead Or Is The Godhead in Jesus?*, makes the following statement: "Joseph was not the father of Jesus. He was the reputed father only. It was the eternal Spirit that performed that miracle act of paternity upon the virgin womb."[1]

However, we must not fail to remember that even though Jesus was fathered by the Holy Spirit, He nevertheless had human limitations. These limitations were present because Jesus willed them so. In order to become that perfect redemptive sacrifice, Jesus had to be tempted by and overcome all the enticements common to man. He had to possess the inherent limitations of man that have a tendency to give vent to the carnal desires. "For since by man came death, by man came also the resurrection of the dead" (I Corinthians 15:21). Jesus had to be tempted by, yet overcome the same temptations that had caused Adam to fall. And Jesus did just that!

From the scriptures dealing with the Sonship of Jesus, two things come into prominence—humanity and time. For example, we read in Luke 2:40, "And the child grew, and waxed strong in the spirit, filled with wisdom: and the grace of God was upon him." Going to Mark 13:32 we read, "But of that day and that hour knoweth no man, no, not the angels which are in heaven, neither the Son, but the Father." This scripture is not a testimony to an all-knowing First Person in the Godhead and a Second Person who has partial knowledge, but rather a testimony to the fact that God, in filling the role of Sonship, chose to limit His knowledge so that He might *perfectly* fill the role of Redeemer. Jesus was the Son of Man because He was born of Mary. He was the Son of God because He was fathered by the Holy Ghost.

He Learned

As the Son, Jesus learned. We find the following in Hebrews 5:8 :"Though he were a Son, yet learned he obedience by the things which he suffered." The very fact that Jesus had to *learn* attests to the humanity of the Son of Man. As the Son of Man we have record that he grew and waxed strong just as any other boy would do. No doubt He also learned the carpentry trade from His reputed father Joseph, as it was the custom in that day for a son to follow in the vocational footsteps of his father. As the Son of God, Jesus also learned. By this statement it is not meant that He became more spiritual, or more knowledgeable of the things of God. For, at the age of twelve we find Him in the temple astounding the doctors with His knowledge. Upon being rebuked by His mother for tarrying in Jerusalem, Jesus answered, "How is it that ye sought me? wist ye not that I must be about my Father's business?" Needless to say, Jesus was not speaking about the carpentry trade.

So we see that at a very early age Jesus was fully aware of His mission here on earth. The learning that took place was actually that of learning empathy. For by suffering Himself, He was able to be a more perfect sacrifice for a suffering mankind. He had to learn on a personal basis what it was like to live the life of humanity. Once this was accomplished, and all the temptations of man were met and defeated, Jesus became that Lamb without spot or blemish—perfect for the eternal sacrifice.

That Jesus Is the Son

He Prayed

As the Son, Jesus prayed. He prayed to the Father because He had willed that the Sonship be a subordinate position to the Father. In Its humanity, the Sonship was limited, but the Fatherhood remained omnipotent, omnipresent, and omniscient. In John 11:41 we find Jesus praying to and acknowledging His dependence upon the Father for power. The verse reads, "Father, I thank thee that thou hast heard me." In various scriptures we find that Jesus took Himself aside to pray. This was both possible and necessary because that He had willed that the role of Son be dependent upon the Father. The entire seventeenth chapter of John is dedicated to a prayer in the life of Jesus. This chapter comprises approximately three percent of the Book of John. If in writing your biography, the author devoted three percent of the space to a prayer you had prayed, would it not indicate a strong dependence on communicating with God through prayer?

Thus, by John devoting an entire chapter to a prayer in the life of Jesus, we are safe in assuming that prayer was very important in the life of our Savior. John was a very close disciple of Jesus. He knew perhaps as well as anyone the day-to-day activities of His life. We can surmise that the importance John placed on the prayer life of Jesus attests to the dependence the Son had on the Father. But once again, let us remember that this primary and secondary relationship existed **ONLY** because He willed it so. The Son was not the coeternal subordinate member of the Godhead.

All the Fulness

He Was Tempted

The temptations of Jesus have been briefly mentioned earlier in this chapter, but it is felt that they warrant further and more detailed treatment, as they are so vital to the complete understanding of His humanity. In this section we wish to treat what has become known as "The Temptation." We refer to the three enticements offered by Satan to Jesus just after His forty-day fast in the wilderness. Actually the temptation process started as soon as Jesus began His fast, for we find in Luke 4:1, 2, "And Jesus being full of the Holy Ghost returned from Jordan, and was led by the Spirit into the wilderness, Being forty days tempted of the devil." If the devil had not thought that Jesus would possibly succumb to his temptations, he would not have wasted his time in tempting Him.

We find in I John 2:16 that there are three types of temptation common to man. They are (1) the lust of the flesh, (2) the lust of the eyes, and (3) the pride of life. In the temptation of Eve in the Garden of Eden, we find there three elements of temptation. They are also present in the temptations of Jesus as He emerged from His forty-day fast in the wilderness.

In August of 1973 I was teaching a course in theology to French and Yugoslavian students in Kaiserslautern, West Germany. One of the assignments given to the students was that of writing a short essay comparing the temptation of Eve in the Garden to that of Jesus in the Wilderness. The following essay was written by a French girl. Although it is simple and brief, nevertheless it tells in explicit language the reality of Christ's temptation, and how closely it paralleled that of Eve.

That Jesus Is the Son

"Our first parents were pure when God created them and placed them in the Garden of Eden. There they lived in peace and were clothed with righteousness. God had given them an order: 'Of the fruit of the tree which is in the midst of the garden. . .Ye shall not eat of it, neither shall ye touch it, lest ye die' (Genesis 3:3). But, according to Genesis 3:6, 'when the woman saw that the tree was good for food, and that it was pleasant to the eyes, and a tree to be desired to make one wise, she took of the fruit thereof, and did eat, and gave also unto her husband with her; and he did eat.' The devil had the victory! Eve had fallen into his snare and had sinned. It was no time at all before she caused Adam to sin also. Suddenly both Adam and Eve lost their cloak of righteousness, and realized that they were naked. As a result, the blood of an animal had to be shed to provide a covering for their bodies. Their line of communication with God had been broken.

"Jesus also was tempted of the devil, but unlike Eve, He did not fall victim to the temptation. Had He been defeated by the devil, His death would not have provided the redemption mankind was in need of. It is interesting to note that Jesus used the Word of God to resist the attempts of Satan. The testing of Jesus was similar to that of Eve in that all three classifications of temptation were employed. In both temptations we find (1) the lust of the flesh, (2) the lust of the eyes, and (3) the pride of life.

"Eve could not resist the lust of the flesh (the tree was good for food), the lust of the eyes (the tree was pleasant to the eyes), and the pride of life (the tree was one desired to make one wise). She was therefore defeated by Satan on three different counts.

"Christ was also tempted regarding the lust of the

flesh ('If thou be the Son of God, command this stone that it be made bread.'). He was tempted regarding the lust of the eyes ('And the devil, taking him up into an high mountain, shewed unto him all the kingdoms of the world in a moment of time. And the devil said unto him, All this power will I give thee, and the glory of them: for that is delivered unto me; and to whomsoever I will give it. It thou therefore wilt worship me, all shall be thine.'). And finally Jesus was tempted regarding the pride of life ('And he brought him to Jerusalem, and set him on a pinnacle of the temple, and said unto him, If thou be the Son of God, cast thyself down from hence.').

"The two temptations were identical, but the results were as diverse as could possibly be. One testifies of complete defeat, while the other displays complete victory. Eve doubted the Word, and fell under the pressure of temptation. Jesus *USED* the Word of God to resist the devil and the temptations he offered. The devil asked Eve, 'hath God said,' while Jesus said to Satan, 'God hath said.' We are reminded of the words of the Psalmist when he wrote, 'Thy word have I hid in mine heart, that I might not sin against thee' (Psalm 119:11). Adam and Eve had lost Paradise by falling victim to the lures of the devil, and being disobedient to the commandments of God. Jesus, in being totally obedient to God's will, was able to restore *Paradise Lost.*"

His Temptation Was Real

The foregoing essay, translated from French, shows in very concise terms that the temptations of Jesus were real. Once again, they were real because He willed it so. It's true that He could have at any

That Jesus Is the Son

time utilized the full power of the Godhead in defeating the wiles of Satan. However, if this would have been done, Jesus would not have been able to become that spotless Lamb needed for the sacrifice and the redemption of man. To undo the damage done by Adam and Eve, He had to be just as they were—except be able to overcome the temptations of the devil. God the Father could not be tried or tempted, but in His role as Jesus the Son, it was not only possible, but quite necessary.

In order to become the Lamb, God had to robe Himself in the flesh of mankind. In Genesis 22:8 we read, "And Abraham said, My son, God will provide himself a lamb for a burnt offering." Although this scripture was speaking of a situation at hand, it was also prophesying of an event that would take place some 2000 years later. In fulfillment of this prophecy we go to the words of John 8:56, where we read, "Your father Abraham rejoiced to see my day: and he saw it, and was glad."

From the very moment of the Fall of Man, God had a plan for redemption. His plan was very simple—He would manifest Himself in flesh and allow Himself to be subject to the same temptations that Adam and Eve had been defeated by. After thirty-three and one-half years of trials and temptation, He would exit from this world totally victorious over *"the very best"* Satan had to offer. We should not think for one moment that His trials and temptations began only after His baptism by John. I cannot help but believe that His entire life was one temptation after the other. "For we have not an high priest which cannot be touched with the feeling of our infirmities; but was in all points tempted like as we are, yet without sin" (Hebrews 4:15).

All the Fulness

Of all the scriptures pointing out the Oneness of the Godhead, the linking of John 1:1 and John 1:14 is the most convincing. John 1:1 reads, "In the beginning was the Word, and the Word was with God, and the Word was God." Going to John 1:14, we discover that, "The Word was made flesh, and dwelt among us, (and we beheld his glory, the glory as of the only begotten of the Father,) full of grace and truth." By adding to this Hebrews 2:14 we are presented with an airtight case. It reads: "Forasmuch then as the children are partakers of flesh and blood, he also himself likewise took part of the same; that through death he might destroy him that had the power of death, that is, the devil."

God fulfilled His own plan by taking upon Himself the form of a man. He became that Lamb that was without spot or blemish. When John looked upon Jesus, and said, "Behold the Lamb of God!" he was looking at God the Father who had decided to become the Son so that mankind could be redeemed.

Limited Knowledge

Upon closely examining the Holy Scripture, we are made aware that as the Son, Jesus had a limited knowledge. Once again we repeat that this condition existed only because God allowed it to exist. This relationship is not to be interpreted as a superior-inferior relationship regarding knowledge. As the Father, Jesus knew all. As the Son, Jesus had limited knowledge. Apologizing for being repetitious, let me once more add that this limited condition was necessary in order for Jesus the Son to become that Redemptive Lamb.

Going to Mark 13:32, a scripture previously used

in conjunction with the section, "His Limited Humanity," we present perhaps the most outstanding proof available concerning His limited knowledge. It reads, "But of that day and that hour knoweth no man, no, not the angels which are in heaven, neither the Son, but the Father." So we see from this verse that as the Son, Jesus was not aware of the precise moment of His return. *The Moffatt Translation* offers perhaps a more easily understood interpretation of this particular verse: "Now no one knows anything of that day or hour, not even the angels in heaven, not even the Son, but only the Father."

It is most interesting to back up one verse to Mark 13:31, where we read, "Heaven and earth shall pass away: but my words shall not pass away." Thus, we find the Son, who in the next verse will say that He does not know all things, stating that His words will stand for all time. If we insist on confining Jesus to the role of Son, then we shall have difficulty explaining the apparent contradiction between verses 31 and 32. How can the Son have limited knowledge of the latter days, yet be assured that the end-time signs He has just mentioned will stand true? Understanding that Jesus the Son is also God the Father, and that as the Son, he chose to limit His knowledge, offers a perfect explanation to the supposed incongruity.

By properly understanding the relationship between the aforementioned verses, our comprehension of many other scriptures should be greatly sharpened. For example: "The Father loveth the Son, and hath given all things into his hand" (John 3:35) or "And hath given him authority to execute judgment also, because he is the Son of man" (John 5:27). We see two things from these verses: (1) The

All the Fulness

Son had a great amount of power and authority, and (2) This power and authority was delegated to Him by the Father. the greater always delegates authority to the lesser. In John 5:36 Jesus speaks of, ". . .the works which the Father hath given me to finish." And in John 13:3 we find, "Jesus knowing that the Father had given all things into his hands, and that he was come from God, and went to God." This is Jesus in His role as Son.

We are not attempting to in any way diminish the supreme and absolute deity of Jesus by inquiring into His Scriptural position as the Son. We are simply showing that the Bible does not present Him as an eternal Son. In so doing, we are not taking away from the deity of Jesus, but adding to it. We are taking away His *coeternal Son status*, but replacing it with His *Fulness of the Godhead status*. We are re-discovering what the Bible says about the special role played by the Sonship—that of providing eternal redemption for mankind.

The Son As To Time

The fact that the Sonship of Jesus is related to time and not eternity is distinctly proven from Hebrews 1:5: "For unto which of the angels said he at any time, Thou art my Son, this day have I begotten thee? And again, I will be to him a Father, and he shall be to me a Son?" The words "this day" can not possibly have a connotation relating to eternity. They speak loud and clear of time, and all the limitations that are included with time. Time has a definite beginning—so did the Sonship of Jesus Christ. For the Word of God says, "This day have I begotten thee" (Hebrews 1:5).

That Jesus Is the Son

This fact is plainly taught by the Bible. Any attempt to teach otherwise can only be the attempts of man to defend tradition. We refer back to the words of Jesus in Mark 13:31, in which He says, "Heaven and earth shall pass away: but my words shall not pass away." Although these inspired words of our Savior were related directly to the end-time prophecy of that particular chapter, I cannot help but believe that this is true of all the sayings of our Lord, as well as the entire Word of God. The Word of God will be standing long after the traditions of man have crumbled to the ground, and have been blown to the four corners of the earth.

I CORINTHIANS 15:27, 28

"For he hath put all things under his feet. But when he saith all things are put under him, it is manifest that he is excepted, which did put all things under him. And when all things shall be subdued unto him, then shall the Son also himself be subject unto him that put all things under him, that God may be all in all."

Before moving into a complete explanation of the above verses, let us remember that the Scriptures declare that Jesus Christ is not only the Son, but He is "all, and in all" (Colossians 3:11) as well. The following scriptures add authority to this proclamation. In Ephesians 1:23 we find the following terminology: "Which is his body, the fulness of him that filleth all in all." Going to Colossians 1:17 we find, "And he is before all things, and by him all things consist." The next two verses, Colossians 1:18, 19 read, "And he is the head of the body, the

All the Fulness

church: who is the beginning, the firstborn from the dead; that in all things he might have the preeminence. For it pleased the Father that in him should all fulness dwell." Colossians 2:9, a very familiar passage, reads, "For in him dwelleth all the fulness of the Godhead bodily." And the following verse (Colossians 2:10) refers to Jesus as, "the head of all principality and power." And of course, we have the passage found in Romans 9:5, which says, "Whose are the fathers, and of whom as concerning the flesh Christ came, who is over all, God blessed for ever. Amen."

From the previous verses it would appear that Jesus is "All, And In All," and that He "Filleth All In All." But, according to I Corinthians 15:27, 28 we find that the Sonship will one day end so that the Father can be *All in All*. Thus, the purpose of the Sonship would have terminated, and the Son would become subject to, and under the authority of the Father. A contradiction exists here only if we attempt to make Jesus a coeternal second member of the triune Godhead. If we fully realize that Jesus Christ is also God the Father, then complete harmony exists among all the scriptures previously quoted.

Surely it is clear from I Corinthians 15:27, 28 that Christ's deity is not dependent upon His Sonship. If it is, then we must be willing to admit that the deity of Christ is not permanent or eternal. It is imperative that we view the Sonship in its true Scriptural perspective if we are going to receive an unobstructed panorama of His deity. If the aforementioned verses state anything, it is that the deity of Christ lies not in His Sonship. Instead, His deity is fully dependent on His being the *All In All, The Mighty God, The Everlasting Father.* These attributes are eternal and are the direct causes of His deity.

The Amplified Bible gives the following translation for John 5:30: "I am able to do nothing from Myself—independently, of My own accord; but as I am taught by God and as I get His orders. [I decide as I am bidden to decide. As the voice comes to Me, so I give a decision.] Even as I hear, I judge and My judgment is right (just, righteous), because I do not seek or consult My own will—I have no desire to do what is pleasing to Myself, My own aim, My own purpose—but only the will and pleasure of the Father Who sent Me."

Surely, this verse must prove once and for all the subordinate position held by the Sonship. But we must never forget that in lowering the authority and power of the Sonship, we are not lowering the authority and power of the Son. For, anything the Son lost in the Sonship, He regained or retained in the Fatherhood.

---

[1] *Is Jesus In The Godhead, Or Is The Godhead In Jesus?* by Gordon Magee, p. 13.

4

THAT JESUS IS THE FATHER

In 1905 the late Sydney Collet's book, *The Scripture of Truth*, was published in Great Britian by Marshall, Morgan, and Scott. Subsequent editions were published by Zondervan Publishing in the United States. Special editions were issued in China, India, Japan, Norway, Spain, and Sweden. It was also released in a Braille edition. From the moment of its initial publication, it became a popular volume, and was considered by most ministers to be quite authoritative. It can still be found in many ministerial libraries today.

The book was not written to present any particular dogma, nor to defend or outline the theological approach of any religious denomination. It was written purely and simply in opposition to the modernistic and materialistic views that were creeping into Christendom around the turn of the century. In the Preface to the 1935 Edition Collett said, "The continued demands for this book are proof that there are yet many who love the old paths, and refuse to give up their faith in the Bible as the inspired Word of God, in spite of the false teaching, and consequent materialism and careless indifference, which abound on every hand today...this present edition is now sent forth with renewed prayer that God will graciously continue to use it for His glory, as a witness to the truth of His Word, in an age of doubt and unbelief, in strengthening the faith of His own people." So, we see from the author's preface to his work that the book is a defense for the Bible and its authenticity.

Before we go more deeply into a discussion of Sydney Collett's work, it might be proper to inform the reader that Collett was a traditional Trinitarian, and did not espouse the belief in the *absolute deity of Jesus Christ.*

The Seventeenth Edition of the book contained 324 pages, 84 of which were devoted to a rather lengthy chapter entitled, "Inspiration." From page 98, which is contained in this chapter, I quote the author. "There is, however, abroad among the critics a blasphemous suggestion that our Lord's testimony on this subject (Inspiration) is invalidated, because they dare to say He partook of ignorance and shared in the prejudices of His Day! To support their theory they refer to Mark 13:26 where Christ, speaking of His own return (Mark 13:32 says, according to the authorized translation, 'But of that day and hour knoweth no man, no, not the angels, which are in heaven, neither the Son, but the Father!

"It ought, however, to be more widely known that the Greek translation for the word 'but' consists of two words, the simple English of which is 'if not'—thus, ei = if, and me = not. The late Archbishop Trench, one of the greatest authorities on words,

All the Fulness

when lecturing to a London College, called attention to this about seventy years ago;* and it can be seen by anyone on reference to a good Greek Lexicon. So that the clause should read, 'Neither the Son *IF NOT* the Father.' In other words, 'If I were not God *as well as man*, even I should not know.' We have exactly the same thought in John 9:33, where these two Greek words are rightly translated 'if not,' viz., '(ei) *If* this Man were (*me*) *not* of God, He could do nothing.'

"This is, I believe, the *CORRECT READING* of this much misunderstood passage, in which there seems to be a distinct reference to the Messiah's title in Isaiah 9:6, 'The Everlasting Father.' And hence *THE LITERAL TRUTH* of Christ's words, 'He that hath seen me hath seen the Father' (John 14:9)."

The preceding statement, along with its conclusion is absolutely amazing when we realize that it was made by a noted theologian who was an avowed Trinitarian. However, in this treatise he was defending the Bible and not the trinity. We find that his defense of the Word of God was made at the expense of the trinity, as he was forced to attack the trinity in order to prove his point regarding the authenticity and infallibility of the Scripture.

In the last chapter, in discussing the limited knowledge of the Son, reference was made to Mark 13:32. Sydney Collett, in paraphrasing the statement made by Jesus in this verse said, "If I were not God as well as man, even I should not know." Thus, he is admitting that as the Son, Jesus did not know all things. It is also implied admission that His absolute deity was not at all dependent upon His being the Son. Further, it is an admission that His Sonship was concerned with His humanity and manhood, and that we therefore cannot *scripturally*

---

*About 1865

That Jesus Is the Father

refer to Him as the Eternal Son.

We have seen from the last chapter, as well as the early stages of this present chapter, that in His great role as the Son, the supreme deity of God was not displayed. This fact is due to the numerous and most obvious limitations which were a part of His Sonship. Jesus' very own statements prove this to be so. And as Sydney Collett said, it is only as the Father that He is shown forth as Eternal God. This is certainly in accordance with Scripture, and the great truth is superbly demonstrated by the following scriptures.

ISAIAH 9 AND JOHN 14

Earlier in the chapter Sydney Collett made reference to Isaiah 9 and John 14. We will now look into these scriptures in depth. Isaiah 9:6, which has been quoted previously in the book, reads "For unto us a child is born, unto us a son is given: and the government shall be upon his shoulder: and his name shall be called Wonderful, Counsellor, The mighty God, The everlasting Father, The Prince of Peace." In this portion of scripture we have an inspired insight into both the humanity and deity of God. The Child born was also the Mighty God. The Son given was also the Everlasting Father. And so it happened that when Jesus reached manhood, and was involved in His earthly ministry, that He said concerning not another, but Himself, "He that hath seen me hath seen the Father."

It was mentioned in the second chapter, "That Jesus Is God," that we would in this chapter return to the portion of scripture found in John 14. In John 14:8 Philip said to Jesus, "Lord, shew us the Father, and it

All the Fulness

sufficeth us." From this verse we see that Philip is aware of the special efforts the Lord has been taking in the instruction of His disciples. While Jesus often taught the multitudes with the help of parables, it was only later, in private sessions that the meaning of these parables was fully explained.

We can be certain that the Chosen Twelve were constantly asking Jesus questions, and seeking a further clarification of the things He shared with them. Seemingly Philip was saying, "Lord, if you will just show us the Father, we will be satisfied, and won't continue to bother you with questions."

In Matthew 13:10-17 we find Jesus telling the disciples why He chose to use parables in His public teaching. "And the disciples came, and said unto him, Why speakest thou unto them in parables? He answered and said unto them, Because it is given unto you to know the mysteries of the kingdom of heaven, but to them it is not given...Therefore speak I to them in parables: because they seeing see not; and hearing they hear not, neither do they understand...But blessed are your eyes, for they see: and your ears, for they hear. Verily I say unto you, That many prophets and righteous men have desired to see those thing which ye see, and have not seen them; and to hear those things which ye hear, and have not heard them."

So, in John 14 we find that Philip genuinely acknowledged the many things Jesus had taught them and revealed to them in the past. He therefore asked the pertinent question, "Lord, show us (reveal to us) the Father. Do this, and we'll be satisfied, and won't bother you with any more questions." Jesus' answer to Philip was as simple and straightforward as possible: "Have I been so long time with you, and yet

That Jesus Is the Father

hast thou not known me, Philip? he that hath seen me hath seen the Father" (John 14:9). In giving Philip this answer, Jesus was really doing nothing more than paraphrastically repeating the words of Isaiah 9:6, in which we find that the *Child Born* will also be the *Everlasting Father*.

True to the words of Jesus, the multitudes of that day, and especially the religious leaders did not comprehend the teachings of Jesus. They had eyes to see, but they did not see the truths He was expounding. They had ears to hear, but they did not understand the words Jesus spoke to them. The one they had awaited for centuries was there in their very presence, and they did not recognize Him. Even the disciples who had the advantage of spending the better part of three and one-half years with Jesus, and who were privileged to attend His private teaching sessions, did not recognize Him as the Eternal Father until He further clarified it to them.

This lack of understanding has continued on down through the centuries, and sadly enough exists today. Men read His Word, having full access to the abundance of scriptures that point to the absolute deity of Jesus, yet fail to grasp the truth. They have perfect vision, yet they do not see the truth. They have perfect hearing, yet they seemingly cannot hear the message that rings loud and clear.

The message of God's Word is crystal clear, with no attempt at mystification, yet they do not understand. There can be no room for discussion as to what Jesus meant by the statement: "He that hath seen me hath seen the Father." It can mean but one thing—the Son and the Father are one in the same. Some might say that in this statement Jesus was referring to a father-son resemblance. It seems almost senseless to counter such an argument, but how could Jesus (in His fleshly body) possibly resemble a spirit? (See John 4:24.)

THE AMPLIFIED BIBLE

The Amplified Bible has the following translation for John 14:7: "If you had known Me—had learned to recognize Me—you would also have known My Father. From now on you know Him and have seen Him." These words stirred Philip into action, and caused him to make the statement which we find in John 14:8. Returning to *The Amplified Bible*, we quote this statement along with the reply of Jesus. "Philip said to Him, Lord, show us the Father—cause us to see the Father, that is all we ask; then we shall be satisfied. Jesus replied, Have I been with all of you for so long a time and do you not recognize and know Me yet, Philip? Any one who has seen Me has seen the Father. How can you say then, Show us the Father?"

Anyone who has seen Me has seen the Father. What can be more simple? In other words, "when you look at Me, you are looking at the Father. Why do you persist in looking for another source? Anyone who has seen me has already seen the Father. I am the Father, Philip!"

The Amplified Bible goes on to translate John 14:10 in the following manner: "Do you not believe that I am in the Father and that the Father is in me? What I am telling you I do not say on My own authority and of My own accord, but the Father Who lives continually in Me does the works—His miracles, His own deeds of power." Truly, "God was in Christ,

That Jesus Is the Father

reconciling the world unto himself" (II Corinthians 5:19). Jesus plainly told them that as the Son He had no power or authority. His power and authority came only because He was also the Father. As the Son He had come to die.

In these verses Jesus was once again declaring in the most plain and simple terms that as the Son He was both limited and dependent. So, it was the Mighty God that dwelt in the Son that was responsible for the great works performed. However, Jesus was and is that Mighty God. We once again repeat that the Child that was born was also the Everlasting Father.

We shall return once more to John 14, when in the next chapter we discover that Jesus presented His disciples with a total revelation concerning His deity, as He showed them that He was Father, Son, and Holy Spirit—the complete Godhead.

At this point in our study it would be good to remind you that the translations from which we have been quoting come from the pen of men adhering to the trinitarian concept of the Godhead. In their honest attempts at translation, there was no deliberate effort to alter the Scripture in order to present a false doctrine. Thus, the eternal truth of God's Word has been preserved. We have included as an appendix to this book, a short chapter containing quotations from the *New World Translation of the Holy Sciptures*, a Bible published and officially sanctioned by the Watchtower Bible and Tract Society. The scriptures taken from this translation are those which confirm the *supreme and absolute deity* of the Lord Jesus Christ, a fact which the Jehovah's Witnesses deny with great tanacity.

The Word of God is so perfect, and the absolute

All the Fulness

deity of Jesus Christ is so interwoven into it, that a translation compiled by men who deny the deity of Jesus cannot help but proclaim it as a very basic truth. It is most interesting and certainly inspiring to study the various translations and find that they all point to the absolute deity of our Savior. Both those who have been in honest error, and those who have attempted to maliciously destroy the truth, have been unable to do so. The Oneness of God is such a vital part of the entire Bible, that to discount it or destroy it would necessitate a complete alteration of the Word of God.

REVELATION 21:6, 7

When discussing the subject of the Fatherhood of Jesus, we gain insight by going to Revelation 21:6, 7, where we find the following, "And he said unto me, It is done. I am Alpha and Omega, the beginning and the end. I will give unto him that is athirst of the fountain of the water of life freely. He that overcometh shall inherit all things; and I will be his God, and he shall be my son."

Notice the statements made by Jesus in these verses. He says that he is the "Alpha and Omega." He follows this statement by saying that he is "the beginning and the end." Next, He says that He will give "of the water of life freely." Going to John 7:37-39, we find that this action is attributed to the Holy Spirit. But, we're jumping ahead, as this topic will be discussed in the next chapter, "That Jesus Christ Is The Holy Spirit."

Again we say that common sense informs us that there can be but one Alpha and Omega. There can not possibly be but one beginning and ending.

That Jesus Is the Father

And, just how many fathers (other than our earthly father) is it possible for us to have? The answer to this question is found in Malachi 2:10 where we read the following: "Have we not all one father?"

The Weymouth Translation presents Revelation 21:7 as follows, "And I will be his God and he shall be one of My sons." *The Amplified Bible* is also very interesting in its translation: "And I will be a God to him and he shall be My son." *The Jerusalem Bible* states: "And I will be his God and he a son to me."

Going to Hebrews 2:11, we find a verse that might appear as a contradiction upon first glancing at it. The scripture reads, "For both he that sanctifieth and they who are sanctified are all of one: for which cause he is not ashamed to call them brethren." Thus, we find the Bible stating that our Father is also our brother. This apparent disagreement is reconciled when we interpret the verse in Hebrews to be in reference to Jesus in His role as humanity, and the verse in Revelation to refer to His role as deity.

There are many scriptures in the Bible that would appear to present unreconcilable differences unless we rightly divide the Word, and recognize the three manifestations of the One Eternal God. For example, how can we conciliate Hebrews 1:5 which says Jesus was begotten, with Isaiah 9:6 which refers to Him as the Everlasting Father? Or, how can we harmonize Philippians 2:7 which says He was made, with John 1:3 and Colossians 1:16 which say that He made all things? In Luke 2:16 He is referred to as the babe, while Isaiah 9:6 calls him the Mighty God. In Luke 1:35 we find that Jesus had a mother, but in Hebrews 7:3 we discover that He is without father or mother.

In Luke 22:41 Jesus prays as the Son, but in John 14:14 He answers prayer as the Mighty God. Hebrews

All the Fulness

5:8 informs us that He learned, and Mark 13:32 tells us that He was not certain of the time of His return; but in going to Colossians 2:13, we find that He possesses all knowledge. In Matthew 3:16 we learn that Jesus received the Spirit, but in II Corinthians 3:17 we discover that He **IS** the Spirit.

The list of such apparent inconsistencies is almost endless. Viewed incorrectly it would seem that the Word of God is a deliberate attempt at confusing the reader. Looked upon with the proper perspective, however, these scriptures become not a contradiction, but a beautiful testimony to the greatest truth of all time—the true identity of God.*

In viewing the Sonship (Manhood) of Jesus, we are reminded of the words of Matthew 8:27: "What manner of man is this?" No sooner is the question asked, however, than the answer comes ringing back in the form of Colossians 2:9: "For in him dwelleth all the fulness of the Godhead bodily." *Moffatt* translates this verse and the one following in this manner: "It is in Christ that the entire Fulness of deity has settled bodily, it is in him that you reach your full life, and he is the Head of every angelic Ruler and Power." *The Amplified Bible* gives the following remarkable interpretation of the two verses: "For in Him the whole fullness of Deity (the Godhead), continues to dwell in bodily form—giving complete expression of the divine nature. And you are in Him, made full and have come to fullness of life—in Christ you too are filled with the Godhead: Father, Son and Holy Spirit, and reach full spiritual stature. And He is the Head of

---

*I am indebted to Gordon Magee's book, *Is Jesus In The Godhead, Or Is The Godhead In Jesus?*, for many of the scriptures used in the previous discussion.

That Jesus Is the Father

all rule and authority—of every angelic principality and power."

In other words, if we have Christ Jesus, then we have dwelling within us the fulness of the Godhead. How? For in Him dwells all the fulness of the Godhead. Jesus is the Father, Son, and the Holy Spirit.

THE FATHER OF SPIRITS

Colossians 2:10, in making reference to Jesus, calls Him "the head of all principality and power." *Weymouth* gives the following translation: "He is the Lord of all princes and rulers." Then *Moffatt* shows us that this earthly Son is also very much in authority in the spiritual realm: "he is the Head of every angelic Ruler and Power." This is further evidenced by the reading we get from *The Amplified Bible:* "He is the Head of all rule and authority—of every angelic principality and power."

Acceptance of the above scriptures should come readily to all readers—even those claiming to believe in a triune formula. But, how can we possibly reconcile these scriptures which claim that Jesus is the sole authority in the spiritual realm with Hebrews 12:9, which tells us that God is the "Father of spirits?" They cannot be reconciled if we insist on believing that the Son and the Father are two separate beings. If, however, we accept the fact that Jesus is God, then all apparent contradiction disappears.

JOHN 14:20

The Weymouth Translation of John 14:20 reads as follows: "At that time you will know that I am in my

All the Fulness

Father and that you are in me and that I am in you." *The Amplified Bible* gives this interpretation for the same verse: "At that time—when that day comes—you will know [for yourselves] that I am in My Father, and you [are] in Me, and I [am] in you."

In John 12:45 Jesus said, "He that seeth me seeth him that sent me." This verse parallels completely with the words Jesus spoke to Philip in the fourteenth chapter of John: "He that hath seen me hath seen the Father." In the Old Testament there were a number of appearances made by God in temporal or angelic form. An example of this can be seen in Judges 13, where we read the account of an angel appearing unto Manoah and his wife, and informing them that they were to be the parents of a son who would deliver the nation of Israel from the yoke of Philistinian bondage. Reading from Judges 13:21, 22 we find, "But the angel of the Lord did no more appear to Ma-no-ah and to his wife. Then Ma-no-ah knew that he was an angel of the Lord. And Ma-no-ah said unto his wife, We shall surely die, because we have seen God."

Going back to verse 17 of the chapter, we find Manoah questioning the angel regarding his name. In the following verse the angel says, "Why askest thou thus after my name, seeing it is secret?" Notice that the marginal reference gives another translation for the word "secret"—Wonderful. Now notice how the verse reads: "Why askest thou thus after my name, seeing it is Wonderful?" Now compare this to Isaiah 9:6, in which we are told that the child that is to be born will be called "Wonderful, Counsellor, the mighty God. . . ."

According to *Strong's Exhaustive Concordance*,

That Jesus Is the Father

the Hebrew translation of the word "secret" as used in Judges 13:18 is *piliy* or *paliy*. When translated into the English, the meaning can be either "Secret" or "wonderful." We find that *piliy* or *paliy* as used in Judges 13:18 along with *pele* used in Isaiah 9:6 come from the same root word *pala*, meaning "wonderful, hidden, and marvelous."

The instance mentioned in Judges 13 is but one of several examples found in the Old Testament of visitations made by God. In the last century an excellent book entitled *The Christian Verity Stated* was written on the subject of theophanies. Its author, a Reverend Chamberlain, was a convinced Trinitarian, but it is interesting to note that he stated that it is very possible that there are *three manifestations* of the One God. In other words, it is possible that there is one God, who throughout the course of history has played three different roles. We could not agree with him more.

John Paterson, in his book, *God In Christ Jesus*, makes the following statement on page 49 concerning John 10:38 and 14:10: "Extremists have said that 'God died on the Cross'; 'when Jesus was on earth there was no God in heaven'; 'Jesus was His own Father'; 'when Jesus was in the grave heaven was empty'; 'when Jesus prayed He talked to Himself—He prayed, not because He needed to, but merely to give us an example'; 'When the Father spoke out of heaven it was Jesus' own voice'—in other words, He was a ventriloquist! But mark this—**when properly taught,** the doctrine often alluded to as 'Jesus Only,' 'Jesus Name,' or 'Oneness,' is nothing like this. It is NOT Patripassianism—it is NOT teaching that 'the Father **IS** the Son'—but that "the Father is **IN** the Son,' a very different matter."

The Father was **IN** the Son in His entirety. The Son was Absolute Deity as well as perfect and complete humanity. One translation renders Colossians 2:9 as "The complete being of the Godhead dwelling in Him." It is also interesting to note that *The Amplified Bible* translates Isaiah 9:6 to read: "Everlasting Father (of Eternity)." What could be more complete concerning the Fatherhood than that statement? In John 10:30 Jesus declared that He and the Father were one. The attributes of Jehovah God, the Father, are all manifestly declared in Jesus Christ.

Francis H. Derk, in his book entitled *Names And Titles Of Christ*, states in the section labeled *JEHOVAH:* "The great redemptive name of God and interpreted as the 'Self-Existent One,' the 'Absolute,' the 'Cause,' the 'Eternal I AM.' The sacred name of God they would not pronounce lest they violate the third commandment (Ex. 20:7). Instead was substituted *Adonai*, i.e., 'Lord.' This is the Septuagint *Kurios* as in the KJV. The name 'Jehovah' is never applied to a false God as 'El,' nor to any other being except one, the Angel 'Jehovah.' This made Him one with God, and who later was God manifest in the flesh.

"In the Old Testament Messiah is considered as Jehovah because the names given to Him betoken deity, along with the attributes of deity. This is the heart of the Old Testament, and the coming of the Messiah is the coming of Jehovah (Isa. 33:22; 43:11 Jer. 23:5, 6, Zech. 2:10; 9:9). He is the essential, eternal, unchangeable one who reveals Himself in Redemption as His many names indicate. Seeing Jesus we see the Father (John 14:19).

That Jesus Is the Father

"Compare the following:

1. Ps. 45:6-7----------Heb. 1:8-9
2. Ps. 68:18----------Eph. 4:8
3. Ps. 102:25-27----------Heb. 1:10-12
4. Isa. 6:1-5----------John 12:37-41
5. Isa. 40:3----------Matt. 3:3; Luke 1:76; 3:4-6
6. Joel 2:27-32----------Acts 2:16-21
7. Zech. 14:9----------Rev. 11:15
8. Ps. 110----------Matt. 22:41-45
9. Isa. 8:13----------I Pet. 3:15
10. Oba. 21----------Luke 1:32-33
11. Deut. 30:12-14----------Rom. 10:6-11
12. **Isa. 28:16; 49:23----------Rom. 10:11.**"*

Some of these cross references may not be as applicable as Derk would present them, but three of them are particularly good. I wish to draw your attention to references 3, 4, and 12, which I feel serve as excellent additional proofs for the subject we are now discussing—"That Jesus Is The Father."

Cross Reference Number Three

Psalm 102:25-27 reads, "Of old hast thou laid the foundation of the earth: and the heavens are the work of thy hands. They shall perish, but thou shalt endure: yea, all of them shall wax old like a garment; as a vesture shalt thou change them, and they shall be changed: But thou art the same, and thy years shall have no end." As Derk points out, these scriptures apply to Jehovah of the Old Testament. But, in going to Hebrews 1:10-12 of the New Testament, we find

*Reprinted by permission from *Names And Titles Of Christ* by Francis H. Derk, published and copyright 1969, Bethany Fellowship, Inc., Minneapolis, Minnesota 55438.

All the Fulness

that the same qualities and actions are attributed to Jesus. Hebrews 1:10-12 reads as follows: "And, Thou, Lord, in the beginning hast laid the foundation of the earth; and the heavens are the works of thine hands: They shall perish, but thou remainest; and they all shall wax old as doth a garment; And as a vesture shalt thou fold them up, and they shall be changed: but thou art the same, and thy years shall not fail."

Thus, we have two almost identical descriptions—one applied to Jehovah God, and the other applied to the Lord Jesus. Such a comparison can lead us to but one conclusion—Jesus Christ is God.

Cross Reference Number Four

The second set of comparative scriptures that we will discuss links Isaiah 6:1-5 with John 12:37-41. Isaiah 6:1-5 reads, "In the year that king Uz-zi-ah died I saw also the Lord sitting upon a throne, high and lifted up, and his train filled the temple. Above it stood the seraphims: each one had six wings; with twain he covered his face, and with twain he covered his feet, and with twain he did fly. And one cried unto another, and said Holy, holy, holy, is the Lord of hosts: the whole earth is full of his glory. And the posts of the door moved at the voice of him that cried, and the house was filled with smoke. Then said I, woe is me! for I am undone; because I am a man of unclean lips, and I dwell in the midst of a people of unclean lips: for mine eyes have seen the King, the Lord of hosts." Turning now to the New Testament, we compare the verses in Isaiah with those of John 12:41 in which John is speaking of Jesus: "These things said E-sai-as (Isaiah), when he saw his glory, and spake of him." Once again we have an

That Jesus Is the Father

outstanding confirmation of the fact that the human form that spent thirty-three and one-half years on earth was nothing more than a fleshly manifestation of the Almighty God.

Cross Reference Number Twelve

The third comparative confirmation from Derk's list that we will discuss is number 12, in which he compares Isaiah 28:16 and Isaiah 49:23 with Romans 10:11. Isaiah 28:16 reads, "Therefore thus saith the Lord GOD, Behold, I lay in Zion for a foundation a stone, a tried stone, a precious corner stone, a sure foundation: he that believeth shall not make haste." Isaiah 49:23 reads in part as follows: "And thou shalt know that I am the LORD: for they shall not be ashamed that wait for me." Turning to Romans 10:11 we find the prophecy of Isaiah fulfilled when we read in reference to Jesus, "For the scripture saith, Whosoever believeth on him shall not be ashamed."

For some reason, in his treatment of Isaiah 28:16, Derk failed to mention the passage found in I Peter 2:6, 7. I take the liberty of introducing this portion, as I feel that it is the perfect New Testament comparison to the verse in Isaiah. It shines out as just another indisputable proof that Jehovah God became Jesus for the purpose of redemption. I Peter 2:6, 7 reads in the following manner: "Behold, I lay in Sion a chief corner stone, elect, precious: and he that believeth on him shall not be confounded. Unto you therefore which believe he is precious: but unto them which be disobedient, the stone which the builders disallowed, the same is made the head of the corner."

Yes, the Stone of the Old Testament was Jehovah, while the Stone of the New Testament is Jesus. We are speaking of two manifestations of one Stone—not two Stones! The Rock who was Jehovah in the Old Testament became the New Testament Rock, Christ Jesus. Does not the Apostle Paul tell us in I Corinthians 10:4, "that Rock was Christ"?

It is most interesting to note that Francis H. Derk was a dedicated Trinitarian, yet in at least three places in his book he refers to Jesus Christ as the Father.

In the section entitled *ETERNAL*, found on page 31, Derk says, "Micah 5:2. 'Olam' as in Deut. 33:27 and Isa. 9:6 where 'everlasting Father' is 'Father of eternity.' The possessor, originator, and the One who bestows."

In the section entitled *FATHER*, also found on page 31, Derk says, " 'The everlasting Father' (Isa. 9:6; Deut. 32:6; Isa. 8:18; Heb. 2:13). See John 12:36; 14:7-10, 16; 21:5...Jesus addressed His disciples as children (Matt. 15:26; Mark 10:24; John 13:33; 21:5)."

Returning to page 41 of Derk's book, we find the statement, "Seeing Jesus we see the Father (John 14:9)." Then on page 91 under the heading *BRIGHTNESS OF HIS GLORY* we read," 'Effulgence' (Heb. 1:3). An allusion to the sun and its radiance, which effulgence manifests and reveals the sun, inseparable and one with it. Thus Christ reveals God and is eternally One with Him (II Corinthians 4:6). To see Him is to see the Father (John 8:19; 10:30; 14:9; Col. 1:15). Consult 'glory' in the concordance."*

Quoting further from this remarkable book, we turn to a section on pages 152 and 153 entitled, *The Plural Names of God in the Old Testament As Fulfilled in Jesus Christ.* The following list of names is contained in that section of Derk's book.

*Reprinted by permission from *Names And Titles Of Christ* by Francis H. Derk, published and copyright 1969, Bethany Fellowship, Inc., Minneapolis, Minnesota 55438.

That Jesus Is the Father

1. Jehovah-Jireh, "The Lord will provide," i.e., a sacrifice (Genesis 22:8-14) Jehovah-Jesus, "Lamb of God" (John 1:29)

2. Jehovah-Rapha, "I am the Lord that healeth thee" (Exodus 15:23-26) Jehovah-Jesus, the Healer (Matthew 8:16, 17)

3. Jehovah-Nissi, "Jehovah our Banner" (Exodus 17:8-15) Jehovah-Jesus, our "Banner" (John 3:14; 8:28; 12:32-34)

4. Jehovah-M'Kaddesh, Jehovah our "Sanctifier" (Leviticus 20:7, 8; Exodus 31:13; Deuteronomy 14:2)
   Jehovah-Jesus, our "Sanctification" (I Corinthians 1:30; Hebrews 10:10-14; 13:12)

5. Jehovah-Shalom, Jehovah our "Peace" (Judges 6:24)
   Jehovah-Jesus, our "Peace" (Isaiah 9:6; Luke 1:78, 79; 2:14; Ephesians 2:14)

6. Jehovah-Sabaoth, Jehovah of "Hosts" (I Samuel 1:3, 11)
   Jehovah-Jesus, "Lord of Hosts" (Matthew 26:53; Luke 2:13, 14; John 12:41)

7. Jehovah-Elyon, Jehovah "Most High" (Psalm 7:17)
   Jehovah-Jesus, "Most High" (Luke 1:78)

8. Jehovah-Ra-ah, Jehovah my "Shepherd" (Psalm 23:1)
   Jehovah-Jesus, our "Shepherd" (John 10:11)

All the Fulness

9. Jehovah-Tisdkenu, Jehovah our "Righteousness" (Jeremiah 23:5, 6)
Jehovah-Jesus, our "Righteousness" (I Corinthians 1:30)

10. Jehovah-Shammah, Jehovah is "Present" (Ezekiel 48:35)
Jehovah-Jesus, the "Presence" (Matthew 28:20)

11. Jehovah-Jesus, Jehovah-Savior (Matthew 1:18-25)*

It would appear that scriptures such as Isaiah 12:2 should be added to Mr. Derk's final grouping. This verse says in part, "JEHOVAH is my strength and my song; he also is become my salvation." In other words, God has taken upon Himself a temple of flesh. But to be fair to the author, we must mention that after he has expounded and expanded on all the wonderful and descriptive titles of Christ, he does mention Isaiah 12:2 on page 157 of his book.

Under the same heading on page 157, Derk also mentions Isaiah 52:10, a verse which tells us, "The LORD hath made bare his holy arm in the eyes of all the nations; and all the ends of the earth shall see the salvation of our God." Going to Isaiah 53:1, we read, "Who hath believed our report? and to whom is the arm of the LORD revealed?" God's right arm was revealed as His *Strong Arm*, His *Saving Arm*—once again we are jumping ahead of ourselves, as we will treat this subject thoroughly when we discuss "The

*Reprinted by permission from NAMES AND TITLES OF CHRIST by Francis H. Derk, published and copyright 1969, Bethany Fellowship, Inc., Minneapolis, Minnesota 55438.

That Jesus Is the Father

Right Hand of God in Scripture."

Returning to Francis Derk's book, we quote more fully from page 157, where we find some very brilliant comments concerning the topic *JEHOVAH-JESUS*.

"In the name Jehovah, God is revealed in all the majesty, mystery, and magnitude of His redeeming self. Man, the crowning act of His creation, is alone able to understand and comprehend the Infinite and Eternal. According to His promises God reveals Himself in His redemptive names. Gradually unfolding in the passing years, they culminate in 'Jehovah-Jesus.' Thus the ultimate name is the name of redemption.

"Salvation is the great all-inclusive word in the Bible, and all that the names of Jehovah implied and revealed is seen here. The 'ever becoming' 'became,' and is now the 'same yesterday, today and forever.' Some day Israel will see who Jehovah-Jesus really is and accept Him. See Isa. 12:1-6; 43:3; 45:21; Zech. 13:6; 14:16-21; Rom. 9:27; 11:12, 15, 25."*

Note that Derk states that the ultimate or supreme name is Jesus—the Redemptive name. Another writer, William Phillips Hall, came to the same conclusion in his outstanding book entitled *A Remarkable Biblical Discovery*, published in 1929. Hall, who had been President of the American Tract Society, spent twenty years of intensive research prior to writing his book. It was closely scrutinized by the most authoritative Bible scholars of that day, and found to be a masterpiece in biblical accuracy. From pages 77-79 of Hall's book we quote the following:

"The Spirit of Truth—according to the Scrip-

---

*Reprinted by permission from *NAMES AND TITLES OF CHRIST* by Francis H. Derk, published and copyright 1969, Bethany Fellowship, Inc., Minneapolis, Minnesota 55438.

tures—revealed to those apostles and disciples and to the Church of the apostolic age the fact that 'the Name of the Father and of the Son and of the Holy Spirit' is the Name Lord, revealed to mankind, and therefore invokable in prayer and otherwise primarily and always for salvation by mankind only in and through the Name of the Lord Jesus Christ, the Son of God.

"For according to Matthew 28:19 the Lord Jesus Christ commanded His disciples to 'disciple all the nations, baptizing them in the Name of the Father and of the Son and of the Holy Spirit'; but those disciples never used or commanded the use of those words in baptism, according to the Acts and the apostolic Epistles. According to their testimony, which is the testimony of the Holy Spirit, baptism was never commanded nor performed during the apostolic age in (or, with, that is, with the invocation of) any other name than the Name Lord, in and through the Name of the Lord Jesus Christ, the Son of God. And that was doubtless for the reason that, as St. Peter declared: 'There is none other name [than the Name Lord (see Isaiah 43:11, A. V., R. V., and D. V., and Joel 2:32, LXX and D. V.) in the Name of the Lord Jesus Christ (see Acts 2:21, 38, restored; 7:59, 60; 8:16; 9:14, 21; 10:48, restored; 16:31; 22:16; Romans 10:8-15; I Corinthians 1:2; 8:6 and Philippians 2:9-11, R. V. and D. V.)] under heaven given among men in which [or, which, that is, with the invocation—Obviously through repentance and faith—of which] we must be saved' (Acts 4:12, Greek Text).

"It is undeniably evident, according to the Scriptures, that the one Name invoked in baptism for the remission of sins during the apostolic age was the only 'Name under heaven given among men in which

That Jesus Is the Father

we must be saved'; and unless it can be shown from the Scriptures that 'the Name of the Father and of the Son and of the Holy Spirit' is in some sense the only 'Name under heaven given among men in which we must be saved,' the invocation of those words in the rite of baptism is utterly void of any saving effect or significance."

You will notice that Hall, having come so near the complete truth, gently sidesteps the issue when he declares that, "the Name of the Father and of the Son and of the Holy Spirit is the Name *Lord.*" We are made to wonder how Hall could come to such a conclusion, especially in light of the fact that one of his supporting scriptures is the passage found in Philippians 2:9, 10. Quoting from *The Weymouth Translation* we read, "It is in consequence of this that God has also so highly exalted Him, and has conferred on Him the name which is supreme above every other, in order that in the Name of JESUS every knee should bow." It is quite clear from this translation of the verse, as well as other translations, that "The Name Above Every Name" is not Lord, but JESUS. Mr. Hall came so far in his revelation, yet he stopped short of the entire truth. We can only surmise that many years of tradition proved to be too great a barrier for him to completely hurdle.

I JOHN 3:1, 2

The Moffatt Translation of verse one reads as follows: "Think what a love the Father has for us, in letting us be called 'children of God!' And such we are. The world does not recognize us? That is simply because it did not recognize him." In this first verse John is stating that the world in general did not recognize Him who was the Father. When did they not recognize Him? When He robed Himself in the flesh of the Man Christ Jesus, and lived on earth. In John 8:19 Jesus said, "If ye had known me, ye should have known my Father also." To know Jesus was to know the Father also. To have seen Jesus was to have seen the Father also. For, the completeness of the Godhead dwelt within the Sonship, Jesus Christ (John 14:9).

Going to *The Moffatt Translation* of verse two, we find John saying, "We are children of God now, beloved; what we are to be is not apparent yet, but we do know that when he appears we are to be like him—for we are to see him as he is." By taking these two verses together, we learn that the One who is returning is God the Father, the One who was not recognized during His tenure here on earth. We find this great fact verified in Daniel 7:22; Zechariah 14:5; I Timothy 6:14-16; Revelation 22:6, 7, 12, 13, 16, and 20. We are made to wonder just how many are guilty of the mistake made by the men of Jesus' day—not fully recognizing who Jesus is?

JOHN 16:23 AND JOHN 14:14

In John 16:23 Jesus said, "Whatsoever ye shall ask the Father in my name, he will give it you." However, in John 14:14, Jesus said, "If ye shall ask any thing in my name, I will do it." Are we to conclude that two persons are promising to do the same thing?

In a similar vein Jesus declared in John 6:44, "No man can come to me, except the Father which hath sent me draw him." Yet, we read the words of Jesus in John 12:32 which say, "And I, if I be lifted up from the earth, will draw all men unto me." So, once again we

That Jesus Is the Father

seem to have a conflict as to exactly who will perform the act. But all apparent contradiction disappears when we realize that Jesus was not only the Son, but the Father as well.

THE RESURRECTION

The ascription of like actions to the Father and the Son can also be seen in discussing the Resurrection. In Galatians 1:1 we read that God the Father raised Jesus from the dead. This is further confirmed by numerous scriptures such as Acts 2:24, 32; 3:15, 26; 4:10; 5:30; 10:40; 13:30, 33 34,37; 17:31; Romans 4:24; 6:4, 9, 11; 10:9; I Corinthians 6:14; 15:15; II Corinthians 4:14; Galatians 1:1; Ephesians 1:20; Colossians 2:12; I Thessalonians 1:10; and I Peter 1:21.

All the aforementioned scriptures attest to the fact that God the Father raised Jesus from the dead. But, complications appear to rise once more when we read in John 2:19 where Jesus says, "Destroy this temple, and in three days I will raise it up." Going to verse 21 of the same chapter, we find exactly what Jesus meant by this prediction: "But he spake of the temple of his body." In other words, "Go ahead, crucify me, in three days I will raise myself from the dead."

How do we reconcile the fact that in Acts 10:40 we are told that God raised Jesus on the third day, while Jesus says in John 2:19 that He will raise His own body from the dead? Once again, all mystery and apparent contradiction disappear upon our acceptance of the fact that Jesus the Son was also God the Father. Any action that either was responsible for could be attributed to the entire Godhead.

THE SPIRIT AND THE SON AS TO OUR RESURRECTION

In Romans 8:11 we read, "But if the Spirit of him that raised up Jesus from the dead dwell in you, he that raised up Christ from the dead shall also quicken your mortal bodies by his Spirit that dwelleth in you." So, according to this scripture we are raised from the dead to meet the Lord by the power of the Holy Spirit. We read in II Corinthians 3:6 that, "the spirit giveth life." John 6:63 informs us that, "It is the spirit that quickeneth." And in I Peter 3:18, we are reminded of, "Christ...being put to death in the flesh, but quickened by the Spirit."

While John 6:63 tells us that, "the spirit quickeneth," we are told in John 5:21 that, "The Son quickeneth whom he will." And to make matters even more confusing to those espousing a triplicity of Gods, the first portion of John 5:21 tells us that the Father, "quickeneth them." Are we to be quickened three times? Have the three persons in the Godhead drawn lots to see Who quickens who? No, all three references are made to the one Almighty God. He is Father, Son, and Spirit.

Seeing that we have touched upon a new subject, we now move on to the next chapter, which is entitled "That Jesus Is The Holy Spirit."

5

THAT JESUS IS THE HOLY SPIRIT

In II Corinthians 3:17 we read these arresting and outstanding words: "Now the Lord is that Spirit." For comparison and further clarification let us go to additional translations and get their version of this portion of scripture.

From *The Jerusalem Bible* we read II Corinthians 3:15-18: "Yes, even today, whenever Moses is read, the veil is over their minds. It will not be removed until they turn to the Lord. Now this Lord is the Spirit, and where the Spirit of the Lord is, there is freedom. And we, with our unveiled faces reflecting like mirrors the brightness of the Lord, all grow brighter and brighter as we are turned into the image that we reflect; this is the work of the Lord who is the Spirit."

We are told that we reflect the brightness of the Lord like mirrors, and that we shall continue to do so until we are transformed into that image that we now reflect. But, in turning to Romans 8:29, we learn that we are predestinated to be "conformed to the image of his Son." Therefore, since the "Lord is that Spirit,"

All the Fulness

and we are to become as that Spirit someday, and since we are also told that we are predestinated to conform to the image of the Son, we have no alternative but to conclude that Jesus is "That Spirit."

Reading II Corinthians 3:16-18 from *The Amplified Bible* we find, "But whenever a person turns (in repentance) to the Lord the veil is stripped off and taken away. Now the Lord is the Spirit, and where the Spirit of the Lord is, there is liberty—emancipation from bondage, freedom...And all of us, as with unveiled face, [because we] continued to behold [in the Word of God] as in a mirror the glory of the Lord, are constantly being transfigured into His very own image in ever increasing splendor and from one degree of glory to another; [for this comes] from the Lord [Who is] the Spirit."

The Moffatt Translation of II Corinthians 3:16-18 reads in the following manner: "Whenever they turn to the Lord, the veil is removed. ('The Lord' means the Spirit, and wherever the Spirit of the Lord is, there is open freedom.) But we all mirror the glory of the Lord with face unveiled, and so we are being transformed into the same likeness as himself, passing from one glory to another—for this comes of the Lord the Spirit."

Our final reading of II Corinthians 3:16-18 comes from *The Weymouth Translation*: "But whenever the heart of the nation shall have returned to the Lord, the veil will be withdrawn...Now by 'the Lord' is meant the Spirit; and where the Spirit of the Lord is, freedom is enjoyed. And all of us, with unveiled faces, reflecting like bright mirrors the glory of the Lord, are being transformed into the same likeness, from one degree of radiant holiness to another, even as derived from the Lord the Spirit."

That Jesus Is the Holy Spirit

I have refrained from extensive comment on these various translations, feeling that they were quite self-evident in their assertion that Jesus is the Spirit—that is the Holy Spirit which some have attempted to relegate to a third position in the Godhead.

THAT CHRIST IS IN US

From Colossians 1:27 we read, "To whom God would make known what is the riches of the glory of this mystery among the Gentiles; which is Christ in you, the hope of glory." Here we are presented with scripture declaring that Christ is in us, and that it is the presence of Christ within us that gives us hope of glory. From Romans 8:9-11 we read, "Now if any man have not the Spirit of Christ, he is none of his. And if Christ be in you...the Spirit is life...But if the Spirit of him that raised up Jesus from the dead dwell in you, he that raised up Christ from the dead shall also quicken your mortal bodies by his Spirit that dwelleth in you."

According to Colossians 1:27, our hope in the *life to come* is Christ in us. But, according to Romans 8, our hope is in the *Spirit* of Christ in us. The two statements made by Paul are in no way contradictory or confusing—in fact they are most synonymous and interchangeable. Paul is trying to tell us in the most simple language that the Spirit and Christ are one in the same. When we have the Spirit of Christ dwelling within us, we have Christ. We cannot possibly surmise that Paul is trying to tell us that the born-again believer has two-thirds of the Godhead dwelling within him.

It is worth mentioning that the Holy Spirit is also

All the Fulness

called the "Spirit of Christ" in I Peter 1:11. In Philippians 1:19 the Holy Spirit is referred to as "the Spirit of Jesus Christ." The term "Spirit of his Son" is used in Galatians 4:6. And in Acts 16:7 He is called "the Spirit of Jesus" (The American Standard Version).

THE COMFORTER

Most students of the Bible will accept the position that part of John's purpose in writing the gospel was to defend the deity of Jesus Christ. *Weymouth*, in his introduction to the Gospel of John, says, "As to the person of Christ, it must be owned that although the fourth Gospel makes no assertion which contradicts the character of Teacher and Reformer attributed to Christ by the Synoptics, it presents to us a personage so enwrapped in mystery and dignity as altogether to transcend ordinary human nature. This transcendent Personality is indeed the avowed centre of the whole record, and His portrayal is its avowed purpose."

But in his presentation of the full-orbed deity of our Lord, we find strong indications in the Johannine Gospel that he reveals Jesus not only as the Son, but as the Father, as well as the abiding and indwelling Comforter. This approach is further pursued in the Book of Revelation.

In the preceding chapter we saw from John 14:9 that Jesus stated clearly: "Have I been so long among you, and yet you, Philip, do not know me? He who has seen me has seen the Father. How can you ask me, 'Cause us to see the Father'? Do you not believe that I am in the Father and that the Father is in me?" (Weymouth Translation). He was thus revealed as the

That Jesus Is the Holy Spirit

Father as well as the Son. But, He was also revealed as the Holy Spirit. In John 14:17, 18 we read the following: "Even the Spirit of truth; whom the world cannot receive, because it seeth him not, neither knoweth him: but ye know him; for he dwelleth with you, and shall be in you. I will not leave you comfortless: I will come to you."

The preceding is clear-cut and most decisive—Jesus Christ is that Spirit. The verses plainly tell us that Jesus Christ, the one who dwelt among the disciples, but was not recognized by the multitudes of so-called religionist, would in the very near future dwell in them. It is most interesting to note that two verses later Jesus says, "At that day ye shall know that I am in my Father, and ye in me, and I in you" (John 14:20).

Numerous outstanding theologians and writers have admitted that the words of John 14:20 attest to the absolute deity of Jesus Christ. Yet, being bound by years of tradition, they seemingly revert back to a trinitarian concept of the Godhead when asked to express their "official" concept of the relationship between the Father, the Son, and the Holy Spirit.

For years members of the laity, as well as leading theologians, have been perplexed by the apparent disparity between Matthew 28:19, and Acts 2:38. Some, not wishing to adhere to the Words of Peter in Acts 2:38, have been so naive as to state that Peter was mistaken when on the Day of Pentecost he told those gathered that in order to be saved, they must, "Repent, and be baptized...in the name of Jesus Christ for the remission of sins...and receive the gift of the Holy Ghost." For they contend that these words are not in agreement with the commandment in Matthew 28:19 where Jesus told His disciples, "Go ye therefore, and teach all nations, baptizing them in the name of the Father, and of the Son, and of the Holy Ghost." To them, the choice is one of believing the words of Jesus or Peter. If given such a choice, common sense tells us which one to choose.

At the other end of the spectrum are those that cannot accept the baptismal formula supposedly contained in Matthew 28:19. They reason that it does not correlate with the message of Peter. So, since it contradicts what Peter had to say, and seeing that Peter was given the keys to the kingdom, Matthew 28:19 must be spurious scripture.

But, when rightly dividing the Word, there is no reason to believe that either scripture is incorrect. A proper understanding of the two verses shows that they complement each other completely. Jesus told His disciples to baptize in the name of the Father, and of the Son, and of the Holy Ghost. Realizing that the fulness of the Godhead dwelt bodily in Jesus Christ, Peter knew full well that Jesus was the name of the Father, Jesus was the name of the Son, and that Jesus was the name of the Spirit. Therefore, when asked on the Day of Pentecost the necessary steps to salvation, he declared that they must be baptized in the Name of Jesus. Peter had understood the Lord perfectly, and was most obedient in his actions.

We must realize that the words of Matthew 28:19 are a commandment, and not a formula to be repeated in the rite of baptism. No one was baptized in the Book of Matthew in obedience to this commandment. We must go to the Book of Acts to discover the meaning the apostles and disciples got from this commandment of the Lord. In going to the Acts of the Apostles, we see that in every instance of baptism, they were baptized in "the name of the Lord Jesus," or some synonomous method such as "the

That Jesus Is the Holy Spirit

name of Jesus Christ."

We are again reminded of the words of Acts 4:12: "Neither is there salvation in any other: for there is none other name under heaven given among men, whereby we must be saved"; as well as the words of Philippians 2:9, 10: "Wherefore God also hath highly exalted him, and given him a name which is above every name: That at the name of Jesus every knee should bow."

In John 14:23 Jesus said, "If a man love me, he will keep my words: and my Father will love him, and we will come unto him, and make our abode with him." From numerous scriptures we know that it is the Holy Spirit that is the indwelling force in the church during this dispensation. So, it seems natural to draw the conclusion from this verse that the Father and the Son are *One* with the Holy Spirit. To make such an assumption is altogether scriptural. When the Holy Spirit inhabits our soul, we also have the presence of the Father and the Son. They are one in the same, and absolutely inseparable.

ANOTHER COMFORTER

Reading from John 14:16, we find the following words of Jesus: "And I will pray the Father, and he shall give you another Comforter, that he may abide with you for ever." *The Moffatt Translation* translates the verse, "And I will ask the Father to give you another Helper to be with you for ever, even the Spirit of truth." Going to *The Amplified Bible*, we read, "And I will ask the Father, and He will give you another Comforter (Counselor, Helper, Intercessor, Advocate, Strengthener and Standby) that He may remain with you forever." *The Amplified Bible* takes the Greek word "parakletos," and uses the various English translations. *The Weymouth Translation* simply uses the term "Advocate" in place of the term "Comforter" found in the *King James Version*.

Going to the next verse of John 14, we read, "Even the Spirit of truth; whom the world cannot receive, because it seeth him not, neither knoweth him: but ye know him; for he dwelleth with you, and shall be in you." In this passage of scripture Jesus was speaking of Himself. "He was in the world, and the world was made by him, and the world knew him not" (John 1:10). Being blind, and not realizing just who Jesus was, the multitudes did not receive Him as the Messiah. He was there with the disciples in bodily presence, but in the near future the relationship would become much more intimate, as He would dwell in them in the form of the Holy Spirit.

In discussion of the topic of "Another Comforter," we once again encounter an example of an action attributed to two persons. John 14:16 tells us that Jesus will ask the Father to send us a Comforter, but two verses later, Jesus says, "I will not leave you comfortless: I will come to you." Are we to expect two Comforters? Is Jesus returning to assist the Comforter sent by the Father? If we fail to recognize the absolute deity of Jesus, we are doomed to a state of total perplexity and confusion.

To further substantiate what we are saying, let us go to II Corinthians 6:16, where we read, "And what agreement hath the temple of God with idols? for ye are the temple of the living God; as God hath said, I will dwell in them, and walk in them; and I will be their God, and they shall be my people." So, here we have it in a nutshell—the Holy Ghost is the

That Jesus Is the Holy Spirit

Comforter, Jesus says that He is the Comforter, and God the Father says that He will personally dwell in the hearts of the people. Yes, when we have the Spirit as an indwelling force, we automatically have the Father and the Son as well.

Let us again consider the conception and birth of our Lord Jesus Christ. We return to a quote from Gordon Magee in his book *Is Jesus In The Godhead Or Is The Godhead In Jesus?* "It was the eternal Spirit that performed that miracle act of paternity upon the virgin womb. The Holy Ghost was a Father to Jesus and that Holy Ghost (the eternal God Who fathered Him) indwelt Him." It would seem from this that The Holy Spirit was the Father of Jesus. But, Jesus tells us that the Father is going to send the Holy Spirit in His (Jesus') name (John 14:26). And, in Hebrews 1:5, we find that Jesus was begotten of God. Therefore, since Jesus could have but one father, and seeing that both the Holy Spirit and God are given credit for having fathered the Son, They must be one in the same. And, since both the Holy Spirit and Jesus are referred to as the Comforter that shall dwell within us, they must be one in the same. Taking these two together, we find that we cannot possibly separate Father, Son, and Holy Ghost. They are **not** the first, second, and third persons of the triune Godhead—they are three manifestations or offices of the One True Living God. Until Bethlehem the Sonship was still future dated.[1]

HE THAT HATH THE SEVEN SPIRITS

In Revelation 3:1 we read, "And unto the angel of the church in Sardis write; These things saith he that hath the seven Spirits of God, and the seven stars; I

All the Fulness

know thy works, that thou hast a name that thou livest, and art dead." From other verses we know that this verse is making reference to Jesus Christ. From Revelation 1:12, 13 we read the following: "And being turned, I saw seven golden candlesticks; And in the midst of the seven candlesticks one like unto the Son of man." And in verse 16 of the same chapter we find, "And he had in his right hand seven stars." Going to verse 17 and 18 we get still further clarification: "Fear not; I am the first and the last: I am he that liveth, and was dead; and, behold, I am alive for evermore."

Moving ahead to Revelation 5:6, we read the following: "And I beheld, and, lo, in the midst of the throne and of the four beasts, and in the midst of the elders, stood a Lamb as it had been slain, having seven horns and seven eyes, which are the seven Spirits of God sent forth into all the earth." By now, it should be quite obvious that the Scripture states that Jesus Christ is the one that has the Seven Spirits of God. In biblical language the number "seven" speaks of perfection. Thus we find the perfect, all-powerful, all-prevading Spirit of God.

A similar thought seems to present itself when we look at Zechariah 4. Verse 6 of that chapter reads, "Not by might, nor by power, but by my spirit, saith the Lord of hosts." Going to verse 10 we discover, "For who hath despised the day of small things? for they shall rejoice, and shall see the plummet in the hand of Ze-rub-ba-bal with those seven; they are the eyes of the LORD, which run to and fro through the whole earth."

Some might still wonder about the "Seven Spirits of God" as seen in Revelation 5:6. Turning back to Isaiah 11:1, 2 we see a most enlightening scripture: "And there shall come forth a rod out of the stem of

That Jesus Is the Holy Spirit

Jesse, and a Branch shall grow out of his roots: And the spirit of the LORD shall rest upon him, the spirit of wisdom and understanding, the spirit of counsel and might, the spirit of knowledge and of the fear of the LORD."

We know that the rod that shall come from the stem of Jesse is none other than Jesus. The second verse goes on to enumerate the seven Spirits that Jesus will possess. They are:

1. The Spirit of the Lord
2. The Spirit of Wisdom
3. The Spirit of Understanding
4. The Spirit of Counsel
5. The Spirit of Might
6. The Spirit of Knowledge
7. The Spirit of the Fear of the Lord

Returning to *Names And Titles Of Christ* by Francis H. Derk, we quote from page 21: "His Anointed is the One that hath the 'seven Spirits of God,' Seven is the number of fulness, perfection and completion (Isaiah 11:2; Revelation 4:5, 6; John 3:34)."

The following list of scriptures, also taken from page 21 of Derk's book, shows that Jesus Christ possessed the Seven Spirits of God.

1. Spirit of Jehovah (Luke 4:18)
2. Spirit of Wisdom (Luke 2:40; 11:31)
3. Spirit of Understanding (Luke 2:47)
4. Spirit of Counsel (Isa. 9:6; Luke 7:30)
5. Spirit of Might (Matt. 11:20-23; Luke 3:16; 24:19)
6. Spirit of Knowledge (Luke 1:77; John 21:17)
7. Spirit of the Fear of the Lord (Heb. 5:7)*

*Reprinted by permission from *NAMES AND TITLES OF CHRIST* by Francis H. Derk, published and copyright 1969, Bethany Fellowship, Inc., Minneapolis, Minnesota 55438

All the Fulness

Once again we are thankful for the contribution of Mr. Derk to this study. However, as before, it is felt that he has failed to use some of the most outstanding scriptures available to him. For example, on point number five (Spirit of Might) he failed to include Revelation 1:8 which states, "I am Alpha and Omega, the beginning and the ending, saith the Lord, which is, and which was, and which is to come, the Almighty." Nevertheless, we are most grateful for the clarification provided us by Mr. Derk.

"LIVING WATER"

In John 4 we read of Jesus' encounter with the Samaritan woman at Jacob's well. In the course of the conversation, Jesus points to Himself in symbolic language as the "Living Water." As Jesus continues to speak to her figuratively she begins to recognize that He is no ordinary man. Her first suspicion is that Jesus is a prophet, but upon being informed by Jesus that He is the long-awaited Messiah, the woman believes Him.

Going to John 7:37-39 we find a passage of similar nature. Verses 37 and 38 quote Jesus as saying, "If any man thirst, let him come unto me, and drink. He that believeth on me, as the scripture hath said, out of his belly shall flow rivers of living water." Going to the next verse, we read, "(But this spake he of the Spirit, which they that believe on him should receive: for the Holy Ghost was not yet given; because that Jesus was not yet glorified.)"

There is much symbolism contained in the Scripture relating to the "Living Water" of God. In Exodus 17 and Numbers 20 we find accounts of

That Jesus Is the Holy Spirit

Moses striking the rock, and water gushing forth to provide relief for the thirsty Israelites. The water supplied by God was a type of the "Living Water" that was to become available later through Jesus Christ by the infilling of the Holy Spirit. Isaiah 12:3 refers to the, "wells of salvation."

Reading from Isaiah 41:17, 18 we find, "When the poor and needy seek water, and there is none, and their tongue faileth for thirst, I the LORD will hear them, I the God of Israel will not forsake them. I will open rivers in high places, and fountains in the midst of the valleys: I will make the wilderness a pool of water, and the dry land springs of water." Isaiah 44:3 says, "For I will pour water upon him that is thirsty, and floods upon the dry ground: I will pour my spirit upon thy seed, and my blessings upon thy offspring." In Isaiah 55:1 we read, "Ho, every one that thirsteth, come ye to the waters."

From Jeremiah 17:13, we get the following reading: "O LORD, the hope of Israel, all that forsake thee shall be ashamed, and they that depart from me shall be written in the earth, because they have forsaken the LORD, the fountain of living waters." Reading from Zechariah 13:1 we find the following prophecy: "In that day there shall be a fountain opened to the house of David and to the inhabitants of Jerusalem for sin and for uncleanness."

Going to the New Testament, we find the words of Jesus in Matthew 5:6: "Blessed are they which do hunger and thirst after righteousness: for they shall be filled." John 6:35 reads, "I am the bread of life: he that cometh to me shall never hunger; and he that believeth on me shall never thirst." Finally, we read from Revelation 22:1, 2 these beautiful words: "AND he shewed me a pure river of water of life, clear as

All the Fulness

crystal, proceeding out of the throne of God and of the Lamb. In the midst of the street of it, and on either side of the river, was there the tree of life."

The preceding was just a partial listing of the many scriptures that refer to the "Living Water." Even a cursory examination will reveal that a majority of these scriptures are pointing ahead to Jesus Christ as the provider of this ever-satisfying water. Yet, the One who is to supply the water is referred to as the *Lord of Israel.* And to bring everything into perfect focus, we read in John 7:39. "(But this spake he of the Spirit, which they that believe on him should receive. . . .)"

So, we find that the Scripture tells us that the Father, the Son, and the Holy Spirit will provide us with that "Living Water." The Bible does not lead us to believe that there are three suppliers of this "life giving" water. Jesus declared that when He spoke of the water He would provide, He spoke of the "Living Water" that would be supplied by means of the Holy Spirit. Thus, we have just one more testimony to the oneness and absoluteness of the Godhead. Jesus is the Father, Jesus is the Son, and Jesus is the Spirit. He is Lord of all.

THE FATHER OF SPIRITS

In Hebrews 12:9 we read the following: "Furthermore we have had fathers of our flesh which corrected us, and we gave them reverence: shall we not much rather be in subjection unto the Father of spirits, and live?" This brings up a most important question—who is the Father of Spirits?

In Hebrews 9:14 we read the term, "eternal Spirit." The words "Spirit of Jesus Christ" are used in

That Jesus Is the Holy Spirit

Philippians 1:19. I Peter 1:11 refers to "the Spirit of Christ." In Galatians 4:6, we read that, "God hath sent forth the Spirit of his Son." There are numerous references in both the Old and New Testaments to the "Spirit of God." We are reminded in Ephesians 4:4, however, that there is "one Spirit."

Reading from Isaiah 48:16 we find the following: "...and now the LORD GOD, and his Spirit, hath sent me." Words like these never caused Israel to suspect that there was more than one Spirit. We see no evidence of lengthy debates among the prophets and religious leaders as to the number of members in the Godhead. For them, the question was forever settled when God told them: "Hear, O Israel: The LORD our GOD is one LORD" (Deuteronomy 6:4). True Jews have always believed in the *One True Living God*.

So, when we read such phrases as "God is a Spirit"; "Father of spirits"; "Now the Lord is that Spirit" (II Corinthians 3:17); we are not to become confused, thinking there is more than one Spirit. For, the Bible declares in clear, concise language that there is "one Spirit" (Ephesians 4:4).

The original Greek of John 4:24 more accurately reads, "Spirit is God." Thus, since the terms God and Spirit are synonymous, and Deuteronomy 6:4 plainly states that there is but one God, there can be but one Spirit. We can therefore look upon Ephesians 4:4 as a confirmation of the words of God in Deuteronomy 6:4. Just as the "Natural Branch" understood that there was but one God, we, the "Grafted Branch" must understand that there is but one Spirit. He is a Spirit. He is the Father of spirits. He is the Alpha and Omega. He is the beginning and the ending.

But, this all-pervading God became the Babe of

All the Fulness

Bethlehem. Later He would become the Sacrificial Lamb. But, the Word of God lets us know that even while He lay in the manger, He was also the Mighty God, the Everlasting Father, and the Prince of Peace. The Lord our God is one Lord, and we do well to worship Him as being total, complete, and utterally inseparable.

[1] *Is Jesus In The Godhead Or Is The Godhead In Jesus?* by Gordon Magee page 13.

6

ADDITIONAL EVIDENCE

As a final chapter to this book I wish to present what might be termed miscellaneous or additional evidence of the unity of God and the absolute deity of Jesus. There will be an attempt to answer some of the most common objectives to the belief in the Oneness of the Godhead.

THE RIGHT HAND OF GOD

In Acts 7:55 we read that Stephen, "being full of the Holy Ghost, looked up steadfastly into heaven, and saw the glory of God, and Jesus standing on the right hand of God." Next to Matthew 28:19, this scripture has caused perhaps the most confusion over the absolute deity of Jesus. As a result of failure to *rightly divide the Word* many have read this scripture, visualizing Stephen looking up into heaven and viewing the Father sitting on His throne, and the Son standing by His right side.

All the Fulness

How many did Stephen see as he looked up into heaven? John tells us that "no man hath seen God at any time" (John 1:18). We read in I Timothy 6:16, "...which no man can approach unto; whom no man hath seen, nor can see...." I Timothy 1:17 describes God as "eternal, immortal, invisible." John 4:24 informs us that "God is a Spirit." So, how could Stephen possibly see God the Father as he looked up into heaven? The answer is, He didn't. Then what did Stephen see? The Bible says he saw "the **glory** of God, and Jesus **standing on the right hand** of God, not beside God.

Since God is a Spirit, he can not have a right hand in the literal sense. What then, or who then, is the Right Hand of God? To obtain the best answer available, we must go to the most reliable source we possess—the Bible.

In Exodus 15:6 Moses credits the Right Hand of God with delivering Israel from the chariots and swords of Egypt. It would seem absurd to claim that God came to earth in the form of a theophany and with the right hand of this theophany physically parted the waters of the Red Sea. What Israel witnessed was a mighty manifestation of the *power* of God—a manifestation of God's right hand of power. The Right Hand of God speaks of strength. It speaks of the Almighty. To Israel, the Right Hand of God always meant the place of power and glory with God. So, we can be assured that as Stephen looked up into heaven, he saw an exalted and glorified Christ dwelling in the place of all power.

Psalm 98:1 reads, "O SING unto the LORD a new song; for he hath done marvelous things: his right hand, and his holy arm, hath gotten him the victory." Going to Isaiah 53:1, we read the following: "WHO

Additional Evidence

hath believed our report? and to whom is the arm of the LORD revealed?" The next verse tells us in very precise terms that the "Arm of the Lord" is the Messiah, the One who gained victory over sin, death, hell, and the grave. Through His Holy Arm or Right Hand (Jesus) God won the victory.

Jesus, the fleshly manifestation of the Almighty God, was the chosen means for accomplishing the ultimate in the power of God—eternal victory over Satan through the sacrifice of the perfect, unblemished Lamb. But, in stating that Jesus was and is the total power of God, we must be careful not to limit Him to that role alone. For, He is the entirety of God. He is "the King of glory, the LORD strong and mighty, the LORD mighty in battle" (Psalm 24:8).

Isaiah 48 is a most remarkable chapter, being packed with scripture pointing to the unity of the Godhead. Verses 11-13 alone contain a tremendous wealth of insight into the eternal mind and plan of God. From verse 11 we find that God declares, "I will not give my glory to another." So, if there be a separate Son in the Godhead, where did He get His glory? Verse 12 says, "I am he; I am the first, I also am the last." This is merely a reiteration of the words of Deuteronomy 6:4 which says, "Hear O Israel: The LORD our God is one LORD." Going to verse 13, we find the following: "Mine hand also hath laid the foundation of the earth, and my right hand hath spanned the heavens." Taking the liberty of paraphrasing verse 13, we find God saying, "With my right hand (the hand of power) I created the heavens and the earth."

Going to John 1:3, we find that all things were created by the Word, who was God. But, when dropping down to verse 14 of John 1, we discover

All the Fulness

that the Word (God) became flesh (Jesus). So, evidently Jesus created the heavens and the earth. To confirm this supposition, we quote a portion of Colossians 1:16, which tells us in reference to Jesus that, "by him were all things created."

By now the relationship should be crystal clear to us. Everything that was created, was created by the Right Hand of God. Jesus is said to have created everything. Therefore, Jesus is the right hand of God. Jesus is not at the right hand of God, He IS the Right Hand of God. The Right Hand of God is simply the *power* of God. Through Jesus Christ, the unlimited power of God is manifested—He is the power of the unified Godhead. Thus, He could truthfully claim to be the Creator of all.

In Isaiah 59:16 we read, "And he saw that there was no man, and wondered that there was no intercessor: therefore his arm brought salvation unto him; and his righteousness, it sustained." Reading from Isaiah 52:10 we find, "The LORD hath made bare his holy arm in the eyes of all the nations; and all the ends of the earth shall see the salvation of our God." The words of Isaiah 52, which immediately precede the Salvation Chapter (Isaiah 53), are written in prophecy of Jesus. In Isaiah 53, the question is asked: "To whom is the arm of the LORD revealed." Isaiah 52:10 has already answered this question.

In Luke 2:30, Simeon looks upon Jesus in the temple, and exclaims, "For mine eyes have seen thy salvation." As Simeon made this declaration under the unction of the Holy Ghost, he ushered in the fulfillment of the prophecy of Isaiah which said that all nations would look upon the Holy Arm or the Right Hand of God. This they did when they beheld

Additional Evidence

Jesus. The words of God in Isaiah 51:5 are, "My righteousness is near; my salvation is gone forth, and mine arms shall judge the people; the isles shall wait upon me, and on mine arm shall they trust." There can be no doubt—Jesus is God's Right Hand, Jesus is God's Holy Arm, Jesus is the Salvation that has gone forth.

THE NAME "JESUS" IN THE OLD TESTAMENT

In the following paragraphs I wish to present a tract written by Arthur E. Glass which is entitled "Jeshua in the Tenach." We wish to express gratitude to the Osterhaus Publishing House of Minneapolis, Minnesota for granting permission to include this tract.

"In dealing with my Jewish brethren for the past many years in Canada, the United States, Argentina, and Uraguay, I had one great difficulty and it was this, my Jewish people would always fling at me this challenging question: 'If Jesus is our Messiah and the whole Old Testament is about Him, how come His name is never mentioned in it even once?'

"I could never answer it satisfactorily to their way of thinking, and I admit I often wondered why His name was not actually written in the Old Bible. Oh yes, I could show them His divine titles in Isaiah 7:14; 9:6; Jeremiah 23:5, 6 etc., and even the word Messiah (Christ) in several places; but the Hebrew name that would be equal to Jesus, that I could not show. One day the Holy Spirit opened my eyes, and I just shouted with joy. There was the very name Jesus found in the Old Testament about 100 times all the way from Genesis to Habakkuk! Yes, the very word—the very name that the angel Gabriel used in Luke 1:31 when he told Mary about the Son she was to have.

" 'Where do we find that name?' you ask. Here it is beloved; every time the Old Testament uses the word SALVATION (especially with the Hebrew suffix meaning 'my', 'thy', or 'his') with very few exceptions (when the word is impersonal), it is the very identical word YESHA (Jesus) used in Matthew 1:21. Let us remember that the angel who spoke to Mary, and the angel who spoke to Joseph in his dream, did not speak in English, Latin, or Greek, BUT IN **HEBREW**. Neither was Mary, or Joseph, slow to grasp the meaning, and the significance of the Name of this divine Son, and its relation to His character and His work of salvation. For in the Old Testament all great characters were given names with a specific and significant meaning.

Now then, when the angel spoke to Joseph, husband of Mary the mother of our Lord, this is what he really said, and what Joseph actually understood: 'And she shall bring forth a son, and thou shalt call his name YESHA (Salvation); for He shall (salvage, or save) His people from their sins.' After I was converted I saw the whole plan of the Old Testament in that one ineffable and blessed Name. So let us now show how the Hebrew name Yesha (Greek: IESOUS; English: Jesus) is used in the Old Testament.

"When the great patriarch Jacob was ready to depart from this world, he by the Holy Spirit was blessing his sons and prophetically foretelling their future experiences. In verse 18 of Genesis 49 he exclaims; 'I have waited for thy salvation, O LORD!' What he really did say and mean was; 'To Thee Yesha (Jesus), I am looking, O Lord!' or 'In Thee Yesha

Additional Evidence

(Jesus), I am hoping (trusting), O Lord!' That makes much better sense.

"Of course Yesha (Jesus) was the One in whom Jacob was trusting to carry him safely over the chilly waters of the river of death. Jacob was a saved man and did not wait until his dying moments to start trusting in the Lord. He just reminded God that he was trusting in His Yesha (Jesus-Salvation), and at the same time was comforting his own soul.

"In Psalm 9:14 David bursts forth; 'I will rejoice in thy salvation!' What he actually did say and mean was; 'I will rejoice in (with) Thy Yesha (Jesus).'

"Something very interesting occurred one spring in St. Louis. I was visiting in the home of our friends, Mr. and Mrs. Charles Siegelman, and another Jew was present. He claimed Jewish orthodoxy for his creed. Of course the conversation centered upon Him who is the center of all things—Jesus. This good Jewish brother verbally, and in a friendly fashion, most violently opposed the claims of Christ in the Old Testament. His best offensive weapon, he thought, was to fling at me, and at all of us there, the well-known challenge; 'You can't find the name 'Jesus' in the Old Testament.'

"I did not answer him directly, but asked him to translate Isaiah 62:11 for us from the Hebrew Bible. Being a Hebrew scholar he did so with utmost ease, rapidity, and correctness; and here is what and how he translated that text verbatim: "Behold, Jehovah has proclaimed unto the end of the world, Say ye to the daughter of Zion, Behold thy Yesha (Jesus) cometh; behold, His reward is with Him.' Just then he crimsoned as he realized what he had done and how he had played into my hands. He fairly screamed out; No, no, you made me read 'thy Yesha (Jesus) Mr.

All the Fulness

Glass, you tricked me!'

"I said; 'No, I did not trick you, I just had you read the Word of God for yourself. Can't you see that here salvation is a Person and not a thing or an event? He comes; His reward is with Him, and His work before Him.' Then he rushed for his own Old Testament talking frantically away, saying; 'I'm sure mine is different from yours.' And when he found the passage he just dropped like a deflated balloon. His Old Testament was, of course, identical. All he could use as an escape from admitting defeat was to deny divine inspiration of the Book of Isaiah.

"When the aged Simeon came to the temple, led there by the Holy Ghost, and took the baby Jesus in his arms, he said, 'Lord, now lettest thou thy servant depart in peace, according to thy word: For mine eyes have seen thy salvation (Yesha or Jesus)'' (Luke 2:29-30). Certainly! Not only did his eyes see God's Salvation—God's Yesha (Jesus), but he felt Him and touched Him, as his believing heart throbbed with joy and assurance. He felt the throb of the loving heart of God as it throbbed in the heart of the holy infant Jesus.

"And thou shalt call his name Salvation (Yesha-Jesus): for he shall save (salvage) his people from their sins.' "

"MY GOD, MY GOD, WHY HAST THOU FORSAKEN ME?"

Reading from Matthew 27:46 we find, "And about the ninth hour Jesus cried with a loud voice, saying, E-li, E-li, la-ma sa-bach-tha-ni? that is to say, My God, my God, why hast thou forsaken me?" Some have

Additional Evidence

encountered real difficulty in reconciling this *Calvary Cry* of Jesus with the Oneness of the Godhead. To them, it is a last minute appeal from a lower power to a higher power. Thus, they become convinced of at least a second person in the Godhead.

Let us never forget the dual nature of Jesus. He was all God, but at the same time He was all man. When he veiled Himself in the flesh of humanity, He became the Lamb of God. To become the perfect Sacrificial Lamb that was needed for the redemption of mankind, it was necessary that Jesus adopt all the attributes of humanity. We have already discussed how it was necessary for Jesus to be tempted in every manner in which we are tempted. By overcoming these many temptations so typical to man, He was able to become the unblemished Lamb of God. This final appeal at Calvary is an excellent testimony to the absolute humanity of the Man Christ Jesus. As death begins to stake her claim, we see evidence of one of the strongest passions known to man—the will to live. Had Jesus not possessed this intense desire to live, His death would not have been sacrificial, and the redemption of mankind would not have been provided. But, with His dying words, He assured us that the price had been paid—eternal salvation had become a reality through the death of the Lamb of God.

No, the second person in the Godhead was not making an appeal, or questioning the actions of the first person in the Godhead. Jesus was simply presenting evidence for His qualifications as the Sacrificial Lamb.

Some have been so oblivious to the purpose of the Sonship as to describe the ministry of Jesus as a failure. "After all," they contend, "very few really

All the Fulness

believed the message of Jesus or accepted Him as the true Messiah. Why, on several occasions He spoke to crowds numbering in the thousands, yet only a very few cared enough to witness His death on the Cross." Such an opinion is in complete disharmony with the Word of God and purposes of God. Jesus was a man born to die. His role was simple—that of redemption. He came to earth for one purpose, and He satisfied that purpose quite well on Calvary.

He was condemned to die—not for personal sins, but for the sins of the world, past, present, and future. I Peter 2:22 reads, "Who did no sin, neither was guile found in his mouth." Jesus was the sin offering for humanity. He died on our behalf. The perfect life took upon Himself the sin of the world.

In Isaiah 59:2 we find the following: "But your iniquities have separated between you and your God, and your sins have hid his face from you, that he will not hear." This scripture in corroboration with others teaches us that sin separates the sinner from God. God cannot condone or bless sin. It is repulsive to Him in any shape, form, or fashion. The intensity with which God hates sin is well demonstrated by the words of James 2:10: "For whosoever shall keep the whole law, and yet offend in one point, is guilty of all." This hatred of sin on the part of God is further exemplified by Revelation 22:15: "For without are dogs, and sorcerers, and whoremongers, and murderers, and idolaters, and whosoever loveth and maketh a lie." God hates all sin—even those sins that we have labeled as "small."

When the Son became the Sin-bearer, and bore upon Himself the guilt of the whole world, Jehovah God hid His face. When the time came, the punishment and wrath of God was hurled at the

Additional Evidence

Lamb of God, and He was literally forsaken. To make the sacrifice complete and effective, Jesus had to endure the punishment.

Our thoughts are confirmed in going to Habakkuk 1:13: "Thou art of purer eyes than to behold evil, and canst not look on iniquity." It would appear from this verse that God cannot even bear to look upon sin. Some people claim that Jesus only **thought** He was being forsaken. He made a mistake in His state of agonizing pain. It was merely a figment of His imagination. The Word of God would appear as our authoritative source, however. The Bible tells us that as Jesus personally bore the sins of all mankind, He was forsaken by God. Both testaments speak of the Son being forsaken by the Father. From the words of David, in Psalm 22:1, we read the very words that Jesus would cry out on the Cross some 1000 years later.

When Jesus died, the second person in the triune Godhead did not die. But in the same light, it would be incorrect to say that God died on the Cross, for God cannot die. Just as heaven was not vacated by Jesus' presence on earth, God did not die on the Cross; neither was He buried in the tomb provided by Joseph of Arimathaea. It was that perfect humanity, that perfect life conceived by the Holy Ghost, which was offered as a sacrifice on Calvary. It was the Lamb who gave His life for us. But Jesus was not "just" the Lamb. It is more proper to say that "He became the Lamb." Reading from Hebrews 10:5 we find, "Wherefore when he cometh into the world, he saith, Sacrifice and offering thou wouldest not, but a body hast thou prepared me."

Let us return to the words of Jesus in John 2:19: "Destroy this temple, and in three days I will raise it up." We have already discussed verse 21 which informs us that Jesus spoke of the temple of His body, and not of the temple in Jerusalem. When Jesus told those Jewish leaders in John 2 that He would resurrect His body on the third day, He was actually saying that as the Mighty God He would once again inhabit the body He had prepared for the sacrifice.

As long as the Spirit of God dwelt in the body of Jesus, Jesus could not die. Once the Spirit had departed, however, death became a possibility. The resurrection of Jesus Christ was nothing more than a re-entry of the Spirit of God into the body of Jesus Christ. This is not an attempt to over-simplify or play down the miracle of the resurrection, but rather to state that once the Spirit had re-entered the body, death was an impossibility.

Again we ask the question: "Just who raised Jesus from the dead?" In John 2:19 Jesus said that He would raise His own body. Acts 2:24 informs us that God raised Jesus from the dead. In Romans 8:11, we read that Jesus was raised from the dead by the Spirit. So, was Jesus raised from the dead on three different occasions? Or, is it possible that such an act was so difficult that it took the cooperative efforts of all three members of the Godhead? Or, is there any chance that the Father, the Son, and the Spirit are all the same, and that it is a simple act of the same event being reported in three different ways? Scripture would lead us to believe that the later is the case.

Before concluding our study concerning the forsaking of the Lamb by God, let us discuss the position of the scapegoat relative to the Old Testament. In Leviticus 16 the role of the scapegoat is presented to us in the very finest detail. Its relation to the Day of Atonement (both Old and New

Additional Evidence

Testament) is so beautifully narrated in this chapter. The Hebrew word for scapegoat is "azazel," and it means *a goat of departure*.

In Leviticus 16 we notice that there were two goats, and that lots (one lot for the Lord, and the other lot for the scapegoat) were cast upon them. What a similarity—lots were cast at Calvary also. One goat was sacrificed for a sin offering. This was the goat upon which the "Lord's lot" fell. Certainly this is a foreshadowing of one lot that would fall upon Jesus Christ. Leviticus 16:15 reads, "Then shall he kill the goat of the sin offering, that is for the people, and bring his blood within the vail. . .and sprinkle it upon the mercy seat, and before the mercy seat." The New Testament counterpart becomes quite obvious when we read Hebrews 10:19, 20: "Having therefore, brethren, boldness to enter into the holiest by the blood of Jesus, By a new and living way, which he hath consecrated for us, through the veil, that is to say, his flesh."

Returning to Leviticus, we read about the other goat in verses 20-22. Whereas the goat slain (Lord's lot) typifies Christ's death in the manner in which it defends the holiness and righteousness of God as seen in the law, the live goat (scapegoat) typifies the eternal sacrifice for the sins of man. In reference to the scapegoat we read, "He shall bring the live goat: And Aaron shall lay both his hands upon the head of the live goat, and confess over him all the iniquities of the children of Israel. . .and shall send him away by the hand of a fit man into the wilderness: And the goat shall bear upon him all their iniquities into a land not inhabited: and he shall let go the goat in the wilderness."

Jesus became our scapegoat. All the iniquities of

All the Fulness

mankind (eternally) were placed upon His shoulders. As He bore these many sins, He went away, so to speak, *into a land not inhabited*. As the time of death drew near, all men, even those closest to Jesus, forsook him and fled. Finally, as the complete weight of the sins of humanity was placed upon Jesus, God forsook Him also. As God looked away, and the Spirit left, death became a possibility, and the eternal sacrifice could be made.

The Day of Atonement was the most important day in the Hebrew calendar. Today it is called "Yom Kippur." It was on this day that the Arab nations attacked the nation of Israel in 1973. It is often referred to as the "sabbath of sabbaths," and was the only day in which the High Priest was allowed to enter into the Holy of Holies.

Dr. C. I. Scofield, in his notes on Leviticus 16, made the following comment: "The offering of the high priest for himself has no anti-type in Christ (Heb. 7:26, 27). The *typical* interest centers upon the two goats and the high priest...The goat slain (Jehovah's lot) is that aspect of Christ's death which vindicates the holiness and righteousness of God as expressed in the law (Rom. 3:24-26), and is *expiatory*...The Living goat typifies that aspect of Christ's work which puts *away* our sins from before God (Heb. 9:26; Rom. 8:33, 34)...The high priest entering the holiest, typifies Christ entering 'heaven itself' with 'His own blood' for us (Heb. 9:11, 12). His blood makes that to be a 'throne of grace,' and 'mercy seat,' which else must have been a throne of judgment...

"The atonement of Christ, as interpreted by the O.T. sacrificial types, has these necessary elements: (1) It is substitutionary—the offering takes the offerer's place in death. (2) The Law is not evaded but

Additional Evidence

honored—every sacrificial death was an execution of the sentence of the law. (3) The sinlessness of Him who bore our sins is expressed in every animal sacrifice—it must be without blemish. (4) The *effect* of the atoning work of Christ is typified (a) in the promises, 'it shall be forgiven him'; and (b) in the peace-offering, the expression of fellowship—the highest privilege of the saint."

Yes, as Jesus bore the sins of the world, He literally entered a wilderness. As he felt the full load of all the sins of mankind (past, present, and future), He entered into a land that was not inhabited. Thus, it is easy to understand why the Lamb cried unto the Father, "My God, my God, why hast thou forsaken me?"

ELOHIM

The Hebrew word "Elohim" has been bandied about for years by those maintaining a belief in the tri-personal Godhead concept. The vanity of attempting to prove their belief by this method has been pointed out on numerous occasions by eminent Bible scholars. Still, there are those who choose to continue this fruitless line of argument.

"Elohim" is the most frequently used word for God in the Old Testament, being found in excess of 2500 times. According to *Young's Analytical Concordance To The Bible*, the term "Elohim" as used in the Old Testament, applies to "angels" once, to "godesses" twice, to "judges" five times, to "gods in general" 240 times, and to "God" frequently. It also refers to "great" once, to "very great" once, and to "mighty" twice. When this term is used in relation to

All the Fulness

God, it carries the connotation of "EXCEEDING."

Strong, in his *Exhaustive Concordance*, points out that Elohim is the plural of the word "Eloah," which means either a *deity* or *The Deity*. Strong goes on to define Elohim as, "gods in the ordinary sense; but specifically used (in the plural thus, especially with the article) of the supreme God; occasionally applied by way of deference to magistrates; and sometimes as a superlative:—angels, exceeding, God (gods) (-dees, -ly), (very) great, judges, mighty."

So we see that even though the word "Elohim" is most frequently used in making reference to God, its use is not limited to God. Therefore, we cannot say that the attributes of the Godhead are dependent on the properties of this word. The plurality of the word "Elohim" in no way necessitates a plurality in the Godhead!

Most all Bible students who have studied the subject "The Angel of Jehovah," readily confess that this angel, who on various occasions represented Jehovah, was in reality Jehovah himself. Chamberlain, in his book *The Christian Verity Stated*, presents this concept in a most outstanding manner, showing that this is the case all the way from Genesis to Malachi.

John Paterson states the following on pages 45 and 46 of his book *God In Christ Jesus*: " 'Jehovah, the God of Abraham and the God of Isaac' appeared to Jacob at Bethel (Gen. 28:13), and 21 years later 'the angel of God' announced to Jacob that He was 'Jehovah' and 'the God of Bethel' (Gen. 31:3, 11, 13). Shortly after this, 'a man' wrestled with Jacob (Gen. 32:24), and the status of this heavenly messenger is reflected in the words He spoke to Jacob—'as a prince has thou power with GOD and with men, and hast prevailed.' This 'man' is called 'the face of God'

Additional Evidence

(Gen. 32:30) and 'the angel' (Hos. 12:4). Furthermore, 'the angel' is identified with the God of Bethel and is 'even Jehovah, God of hosts' (Hos. 12:4, 5). If further identification is needed it is surely found in the word, 'Jehovah is His memorial' (Hos. 12:5), directing our thoughts to the burning bush where 'I AM' declared Himself 'Jehovah, the God of Jacob: this is MY name for ever, and this is My memorial unto all generations' (Exodus 3:13-15; Acts 7:30, 38). In passing, I might mention that Jacob said of this 'man,' 'I have seen ELOHIM face to face' (Gen. 32:30)...this is not the only place in the Bible where the *plural* Elohim is applied to the singular Christ!"

As stated before, Bible scholars commonly accept the fact that the "Angel of Jehovah" of the Old Testament was the Lord Jesus Christ. But, in maintaining this position, they must also admit that in the light of Genesis 32:30 Jesus is also Elohim. And, if there remains an insistence on the word "Elohim" indicating a plurality of persons in the Godhead, then of necessity Jesus must be all three.

Ralph Vincent Reynolds, on page 9 in his *Alpha Bible Course-Bible Doctrine Part I*, gives us some additional scriptures concerning the word "Elohim" as applied to Jesus Christ. "Elohim is applied to Jesus Christ in the following scriptures:

Zechariah 11:4, 12, 13	Elohim was sold for thirty pieces of silver.
Zechariah 14:5	Elohim is coming back as King.
Zechariah 12:10	Elohim was pierced at Calvary.

Reynold's stand is further confirmed by the following quote found in Smith's Bible Dictionary:

All the Fulness

"The plural form of Elohim was given rise to much discussion. The fanciful idea, that it referred to the Trinity of Persons in the Godhead, hardly finds now a supporter among scholars. It is either what grammarians call the plural of majesty, or it denotes the fulness of divine strength, the sum of powers displayed by God."

But despite the myriad of evidence present, there are those that still insist on a tri-personal God and point to what they consider foolproof evidence—Genesis 1:26, which reads, "And God said, Let us make man in our image, after our likeness." To them, this is a quotation of the Godhead as they discussed plans for the creation of man.

In going to Job 38:7, we discover who in all probability God was conversing with when He shared His plans for the creation of man. The verse reads, "When the morning stars sang together, and all the sons of God shouted for joy." The angels are referred to as "sons of God" in the Old Testament. Here we find the angels praising the creations of God. Most likely, it was with these angels that He discussed His plans to create the first man. We have no basis for believing that the Godhead was having a board meeting.

Gordon Magee has this to say concerning the word "Elohim": "Elohim is translated *God* in our Bibles; it indicates a plurality of attributes and not of persons. Baal (Judges 6:31) and Baalzebub (II Kings 1:2) are called Elohim, but they were not trinities. Great Bible teachers, such as Calvin, have ridiculed the notion that this word affords any support for a belief in Divine persons. Elohim is applied to Christ, thus proving that it does not mean a plurality of persons...Do we think that three persons were

Additional Evidence

betrayed, crucified, and are coming again? Of course not! The very use of the word Elohim in Scripture proves that by it the sacred writers did not mean three Divine persons but rather our one Lord Jesus Christ, Who has *all* the attributes of full-orbed Deity."1

Concerning Genesis 1:26, Magee has this to say: "Trinitarians argue that this verse shows a trinity of Divine persons, but the verse immediately following says, 'God created man in *His* own image, in the image of God created *He* him.' Notice the use of the singular personal pronouns. John 1:3, 10 makes it clear that creation was the work of *One* Divine Person. 'The world was made by Him' (Jesus). Isaiah 44:24 is crystal clear on this point. God speaks in the first person and says, 'I am the LORD...that spreadeth abroad the earth by *Myself.*' Could language be plainer? *Creation* is the work of One Divine *Person only. (See James 2:19; Mal. 2:10.)*

"Angels were present when God made the world (see Job 38:7), and they applauded *His* creative acts. Jehovah converses with angels (see Psalm 103:20). The Jews have always believed that the *us* of Gen. 1:26 refers to God and the angels. A careful study of Gen. 3:22-24, where the *"us"* again appears, reveals that God is addressing the cherubim or elect angels who, together with himself, 'knew good and evil.'...'*Us*' relative to God and the angels, is seen again in Gen. 11:7, where God indicates to the angels that Babel's hour of judgment had come, 'Let *Us* go down and confound them.' As at Sodom, God, in conjunction with the angels, executed the work of vengeance (Gen. 18:33 and 19:1)... Some people see a major objection to all this in Isaiah 40:12, 13. Let them read the passage carefully, it does not clash with

All the Fulness

our proposition, it does not say that God refuses to counsel with angels—it simply states that no one, as His counselor, *teaches or instructs* the Almighty. God does counsel with angels...He even counsels with men. He counselled with Abraham (Gen. 18:17) about Sodom, and not only counselled but permitted the man Abraham to actually *bargain* with Him. Nevertheless, neither Abraham nor the angels ever taught God anything."[2]

The foregoing discussion makes it clear to us that in the past God has revealed to His angels His plans relative to the acts of creation, as well as other major events that affected the course of history. Do we not read in the very first verse of the Book of Revelation that God sent His angel unto John to show him the things that would occur prior to the return of the Lord? And in Revelation 22:16 we find that Jesus sent an angel to testify unto the churches. God does use angels, and in order to use them effectively, it is necessary that He reveal things to them.

In conclusion of this section on the word "Elohim," let me repeat that the grammatical plurality of the word "Elohim" does not in any way indicate or necessitate a plurality of persons in the Godhead. Also, there is nothing contained in the Scripture that would tend to indicate that the word "Elohim" is referring to more than one. The Trinitarian concept of the Godhead is without a morsel of scriptural evidence—it is strictly man-made.

THE PAGAN ORIGIN OF TRINITARIANISM

In June 325 A. D., Constantine the Great, ruler of the Roman Empire, convened the first general council

Additional Evidence

of the "church." It assembled at Nicaea, a small town in Asia Minor, some 45 miles from Constantinople. Three hundred and eighteen bishops attended this council, which was called to discuss the deity of Jesus Christ. The leading figures in this controversy were Arius, who believed that Jesus is *somewhat like God, but not fully God;* and Athanasius, who believed that Jesus is *fully God.* In modern parlance we would refer to Arius as a Unitarian.

Almost all the Bishops attending the meeting from the western part of the empire had by now accepted the doctrine of the trinitarian, tri-personal Godhead. Although not the first to espouse this concept, Tertullian, with his articulate manner of speech and writing, had been able to gain widespread support for this doctrine. But we are told that in the eastern part of the empire much of the church still adhered to the Apostolic concept of the Godhead, which included a belief in the *One True God,* as well as baptism in *The Name of Jesus.*

After meeting for more than two months, a decision was reached in favor of those believing in the trinitarian concept. These bishops were in the majority of course. Thus, the Nicene Creed was composed, and passed upon as the standard of doctrine for the church. This creed, with minor alterations and variations is the creed used by the majority of trinitarian Christendom today. It is not Apostolic, and is in fact a direct departure from Apostolic teachings.

Although the Nicene Creed was not aimed directly at the doctrine of the Oneness of the Godhead, its effects were directly detrimental to the cause of the Apostolic believers, in that it gave the teaching of trinitarianism an official sanction. Thus, we find that little more than three centuries after the church had begun, it was falling headlong into complete apostasy. (See pages 20-25 of Loraine Boettner's book, *Roman Catholicism*.) Jesus said, "Howbeit in vain do they worship me, teaching for doctrines the commandments of men. For laying aside the commandment of God, ye hold the tradition of men...Making the word of God none effect through your tradition" (Mark 7:7, 8, 13). And so we find the majority of Christendom today following the doctrines of man established over 1600 years ago, never questioning them as to their scriptural validity.

The doctrine of the Trinity was introduced about the middle of the second century. As mentioned previously, Tertullian was actually the father of the doctrine, as he was the one who was able to attract a large following. Tertullian is also credited with having introduced the trine formula of baptism which consisted of immersing the candidates three times (once for each member of the Godhead). The Encyclopedia Britannica states that this form of baptism was, "invented to explain an existing custom, which the church had adopted from its pagan medium, for pagan lustrations (purfication ceremonies) were normally three-fold."

Concerning the pagan origin of the trinitarian concept of the Godhead, we quote from a book entitled *The Two Babylons*, by Alexander Hislop. "In the unity of that only God of the Babylonians there were three persons and to symbolize that doctrine of the Trinity, they employed, as the discoveries of Layard prove, the equilateral triangle, just as it is well known the Romish Church does at this day." Hislop goes on to say, "The Papacy has in some of its Churches, as,

Additional Evidence

for instance, in the Monastery of the so-called Trinitarians of Madrid, an image of the Triune God, with three heads and one body. The Babylonians had something the same. Mr. Layard, in his last work, has given a specimen of such a triune divinity, worshipped in ancient Assyria."

No doubt the Babylonians were worshipping such a trinity when the Jews were carried captive there in the seventh century B. C. We find examples of Daniel and the Three Hebrew Children refusing to bow down and worship the Babylonian deity. In going to the Old Testament, we find that God repeatedly warned His people against worshipping the gods of surrounding nations. They were strictly forbidden to participate in any of the idolatrous practices of the pagans.

But, we find that the practices that Judaism refused to conform to were later incorporated into the tenets of the church (that is the Roman Church). Easter is of Babylonish origin, and was introduced in commemoration of the supposed resurrection of Tammuz, the god of fertility. In Babylon it was referred to as the *Feast of Ishtar.* Ishtar was worshipped as the wife of Tammuz. W. Lansdell-Wardle, in his book *Israel and Babylon*, states, "The triad of divinities *Sin, Samash, and Ishtar*, is reckoned in the Pan-Babylonian theory as a family, the children of Anu, the father of the gods."

In Judges 2:13 we read, "And they forsook the LORD, and served Ba-al and Ash-ta-roth." Scofield's notes on this verse read, "Ashtaroth, plural of Ashtoreth (I Ki. 11:5), were figures of Ashtoreth the Phoenician goddess (the Astarte of the Greeks), which were worshipped as idols during times of spiritual declension in Israel (Jud. 10:6; I Sam. 7:3, 4;

12:10; 31:10; I Ki. 11:5, 33; II Ki. 23:13). Jeremiah refers (44:18, 19) to Ashtoreth as th'queen of heaven.'" In his notes on Deuteronomy 16:21, Scofield says, "Ashtoreth, who was the Babylonian goddess *Ishtar,* the *Aphrodite* of the Greeks, the *Venus* of the Romans."

I Samuel 7:3 says, "Put away the strange gods and Ash-ta-roth from among you, and prepare your hearts unto the LORD, and serve him only." See also I Samuel 12:10 and I Samuel 31:10. In I Kings 11:5 we read that Solomon went after Ashtoreth the goddess of the Zidonians. In the next verse we see that this action was considered as evil in the sight of the Lord.

Daniel, along with the other true worshippers of God refused to participate in such worship. They were willing to face the Fiery Furnace or the Den of Lions in order to remain true to Jehovah. It is indeed a shame that so much of Christendom has not been willing to make the same sacrifice or take the same stand.

J. R. Illingworth, in his book entitled *The Doctrine of the Trinity,* written in 1907, defends the tri-personal stand of Athanasuis, but does make the following admission on page 74: "There were trinities, in the sense of three-fold groups among the gods of India; and again among those of ancient Babylonia; and again in Egypt. A philosophic trinity occurs in Plato, and is very prominent in Neoplatonic thought."

---

[1] *Is Jesus In The Godhead, Or Is The Godhead in Jesus?* by Gordon Magee, p. 27
[2] IBID, p. 26

APPENDIX I

THUS SAITH THE JEHOVAH'S WITNESSES

As previously stated, the absolute deity of Jesus Christ is so completely ingrained into the Word of God, that simple alteration will not remove it. To delete the Oneness of the Godhead from the Bible would necessitate such a massive overhaul that it would scarcely be recognized as Scripture once the task was completed. An example of this can be seen from the *New World Translation of the Holy Scripture*, a translation published and officially sanctioned by the Watchtower Bible and Tract Society, publishers for the Jehovah's Witnesses.

The Jehovah's Witnesses, who are Arian or Unitarian in their beliefs, of course deny the absolute deity of Jesus Christ. In fact, they deny that Jesus Christ possessed **any** deity, insisting that He was God's first created, but in no way even a part of the Godhead. Yet, it is a simple matter to prove the absolute deity of our Lord Jesus Christ by using their own translation of the Bible. God has a way of preserving the Truth!

All the Fulness

In the remainder of this section, we shall use quotations from the *New World Translation of the Holy Scripture* to once again show that Jesus Christ is the entirety of the Godhead. Unless otherwise indicated, the scriptures quoted in this section will be from the Jehovah's Witnesses translation.

From Job 19:26, 27 we read the following: "And after my skin, [which] they have skinned off,—this! Yet reduced in my flesh I shall behold God. Whom even I shall behold for myself, And [whom] my very eyes will certainly see, but not some stranger."

Linking the above verse with their translation of I John 3:1, 2, we find, "See what sort of love the Father has given us, so that we should be called children of God; and such we are. That is why the world does not have a knowledge of us, because it has not come to know him. Beloved ones, now we are children of God, but as yet it has not been made manifest what we shall be. We do know that whenever he is made manifest we shall be like him, because we shall see him just as he is."

There is a perfect linking of the two passages. Both Job and John were talking about God the Father. However, we are told that this Deity is going to appear, and that mankind will be able to behold Him. Who is coming back? Acts 1:11 tells us that Jesus is the One who is returning. Who are we going to behold? John 4:24 tells us that God is a Spirit. How can we behold a Spirit? How can we be manifested in likeness of a Spirit? And to make the case even more airtight, we read in Zechariah 12:10 that they will look for the One whom they pierced. Can there be any mystery as to who this could be? It seems quite evident that Job, John, and Zechariah were all looking for the same One to return—Jesus Christ.

Thus Saith the Jehovah's Witnesses

Going to Zechariah 14:3-5 we read, "And Jehovah will certainly go forth and war against those nations as in the day of his warring, in the day of fight. And his feet will actually stand in that day upon the mountain of the olive trees, which is in the front of Jerusalem...And Jehovah my God will certainly come, all the holy ones being with him." According to this translation, it is Jehovah that is returning. But, in going once more to Acts 1:11, we find that Jesus Christ is returning to the Mount of Olives, the exact place that Zechariah gives as the point of return for Jehovah. The conclusion to be drawn from this comparison is quite evident. Our point is only strengthened by quoting Titus 2:13: "While we wait for the happy hope and glorious manifestation of the great God and of [the] Savior of us, Christ Jesus."

From Revelation 22:6, 7 we read, "These words are faithful and true; yes, Jehovah the God of the inspired expressions of the prophets sent his angel forth to show his slaves* the things that must shortly take place. And look! I am coming quickly." Going to verse 12 of the same chapter, we find, " 'Look! I am coming quickly, and the reward I give is with me. . . .' " We now link the two above verses with verse 16 of the same chapter which says, " 'I, Jesus, sent my angel to bear witness to you people of these things for the congregations. . . .' " Finally, in verse 20 we read, " 'Yes; I am coming quickly.' Amen! Come, Lord Jesus."

Once again, from the words of an Arian-Unitarian translation of the Bible, we have positive confirmation of the absolute deity of our Lord Jesus Christ.

In conclusion, we will quote from the first two chapters of Revelation. In Revelation 1:7 we read the

All the Fulness

following: "Look! He is coming with the clouds, and every eye will see him, and those who pierced him; and all the tribes of the earth will beat themselves in grief because of him." Then in the next verse we read, "I am the Alpha and the Omega, says Jehovah God, the One who is and who was and who is coming, the Almighty." So, we see from verse 7 that Jesus is returning, and from verse 8 that Jehovah God is returning. Is there a chance that they are the same?

We see a close comparison of these verses found in Revelation with that of Zechariah 14:5. In Zechariah we read, "And Jehovah my God will certainly come, all the holy ones being with him." But, in going to II Thessalonians 1:7, we find the following: "The Lord Jesus from heaven with his powerful angels."

In Revelation 1:17, 18 we read, "And when I saw him, I fell as dead at his feet. And he laid his right hand upon me and said: 'Do not be fearful. I am the First and the Last, and the living one; and I became dead, but, look! I am living forever and ever, and I have the keys of death and Hades.'" And in Revelation 2:8 it says, "'And to the angel of the congregation in Smyrna write: These are the things that he says, The First and the Last, who became dead and came to life [again].'"

The *New World Translation of the Holy Scriptures* therefore admits that Jesus is the First and the Last. It would be interesting to discover how many firsts and how many lasts the Jehovah's Witnesses would lead us to believe exist. Their very own translation says in Isaiah 48:11, 12, "And to no one else shall I give my own glory. . .I am the first, Moreover I am the last." If Jesus is not Jehovah, then it must be explained to us how He can possibly be the First and the Last. How can a created being be the First?

APPENDIX II

A NINETEENTH CENTURY TESTIMONY

In 1974, Mervyn Miller, a very dear friend and fellow minister, was walking through an abandoned church building in London, England, and came across a book written in 1828 by John Clowes, minister of St. John's Church in Manchester, England. In the next few pages I will take the liberty of quoting from a number of the sermons contained in this volume. It will prove quite enlightening to discover how at least one nineteenth century minister viewed the person of our Lord Jesus Christ. The existence of this book of sermons is proof that he did not harbor these beliefs, but made a public confession of them to his congregation.

From page 9—Clowes makes reference to the Lord Jesus in the following manner: "In other words, from the manifested God, Whose high and holy name is Jesus Christ."

From pages 15 and 16—We read the following: "For what shall we say is involved in the most sacred

All the Fulness

and significant name the Bridegroom, and to whom is the name applied? Everyone knows that the term Bridegroom expresses all that is most endearing in affection, and most honorable and dignified in character. If we look into the Old Testament we shall there find that this most holy and interesting title is assumed by Jehovah Himself to denote the sacred relationship subsisting between Himself and His church, or people, for thus it is written, 'As the Bridegroom rejoiceth over the Bride, so shall thy God rejoice over thee' (Isaiah 62:5). And if we further consult the pages of the New Testament, we shall be further delighted at the discovery that the same holy title is applied to the Great Saviour Jesus Christ, or the Manifested Jehovah. Concerning Whom John the Baptist thus testifies, 'He that hath the bride is the Bridegroom; but the friend of the Bridegroom, which standeth and heareth Him, rejoiceth greatly because of the Bridegroom's voice: This my joy therefore is fulfilled' (John 3:29). Jesus Christ Himself also confirmeth this testimony, where He saith, 'Can the children of the bridechamber mourn whilst the Bridegroom is with them? But the days will come when the Bridegroom shall be taken away from them, and then shall they fast' (Matthew 9:15). In which words it is manifest that this Great Redeeming God assumes the same Divine title of Bridegroom under His revelation of Himself in the flesh...From this combined authority then of evidence, resulting from the express declarations both of the Old and New Testaments, we are fully warranted in establishing the interesting conclusion, first, that the Jehovah of the Old Testament and the Jesus of the New are the same identical Being, differing from each other only as that which is manifested in a body of flesh and blood differs from that which is not so manifested."

From page 18—"Lastly we learn that by the Bridegroom is here meant the Manifested God, Whose high and holy name is Jesus Christ."

From page 21—"When Jesus Christ speaks His voice is the voice of God Himself."

From page 56—"Jesus Christ is the Eternal God made Man."

From page 63—"It will be midnight also with the present christian church should it ever come to pass that this manifested God is either rejected in the church as having no just title to divinity and divine worship, or is acknowledged only partially, in consequence of not being approached and worshipped as the Only God. For if one truth be more to be depended on than another it is that **God Is One,** and that thus it is impossible that there can be more Gods than one. If Jesus Christ be acknowledged to be God He must in such case of necessity be acknowledged to be the only God, and approached and worshipped accordingly, otherwise His divinity is as completely denied and rejected as if He were not approached and worshipped at all."

From page 64—"Multitudes at this day, who still call themselves Christians—acknowledge indeed the divinity of this Saviour, but then they acknowledge it partially, and thus, for want of seeing that He is the only God, since there can be but one God, they do not worship Him as the only God."

From page 137—" 'I and my Father are one' (John 10:30). 'All power is given unto me in heaven and in earth' (Matt. 28:18). 'I am Alpha and Omega,

All the Fulness

the Beginning and the Ending, saith the Lord; which is, and which was, and which is to come, the Almighty' (Rev. 1:8, 11). Thus all the generations of men were henceforth to be taught that in the divine person of Jesus Christ, the Father and the Son, or the Humanity and Divinity, are eternally ONE."

From page 142—"The Father of Mercies, whose High and Holy Name is Jesus Christ."

From pages 227 and 228—The following is excerpted from a sermon preached by Clowes on a Christmas Day: "Turn your eyes then towards yonder Bethlehem, the sacred birth-place of the Incarnate God, and behold in that new-born infant, the descent and approach of all the powers of the Eternal to bless and to save a sinful world...He is God made man, that He might bring near unto man His righteousness and salvation, which man by sin had put away so far from himself...In that Wonderful Child then the Kingdom is brought near and opened for all who wish to enter...For that Child is the Door of the heavenly sheepfold, and whosoever goes in through that door finds pasture."

From page 236—"Accordingly, they who in ancient times prophesied concerning the coming appearances of this Great Incarnate God, were agreed in this testimony respecting Him, that at His approach and manifestation, 'the eyes of the blind should be opened, and they should see the King in His beauty' (Isa. 33:17), that God would destroy in that day the covering that was cast over all people and the vail that was spread over all nations' (Isa. 25:7), that all should rejoice and sing on the occasion, 'Lo, this is our GOD, we have waited for him, and he will save us' (verse 9). To that same purpose that Incarnate God himself testifies, 'He that seeth the Father' (John 14:9)."

From page 239—" 'I and my Father are one; believe me that I am in the Father and the Father in me' (John 10:30; 14:11). Thus by looking at this God-man we behold all the fulness of the Father; by fixing our eyes on the visible Jesus we contemplate the glory, the perfections, the mercy, the truth, and the face of the invisible Deity."

From page 247—"Let us draw nigh I say in the spirit of true repentance, unto Jesus Christ, as to the Visible, the Manifested, the Near, the Omnipotent, the Reconcilable God. Let us believe that in His Divine Person all the fulness of the Godhead dwelleth bodily. Let us adore the merciful and miraculous provision thus made for our salvation."

From pages 431 and 432—"Perhaps you are convinced from the plain testimony of the Sacred Writings that Jesus Christ must be more than a mere man and nothing less than God. Nevertheless possibly you do not yet draw nigh, and come unto Him in your worship, as the supreme object of your adoration. Possibly in your approaches to heaven you address your prayers immediately to another being whom you call the Father, and not directly to Jesus Christ, Whom you regard only as a mediatory, or interceeding God with the Father. But let me admonish you, from the words of my text (Matt. 11:28) to be upon your guard, and to take good heed unto yourselves, in a point so exceedingly interesting, and of so much concern to you. Jesus Christ says expressly, 'Come unto me' and in another place

All the Fulness

'Abide in Me' (John 15:4), and again, 'No man cometh to the Father but by Me' (John 14:6), and lastly, 'He that hath seen me hath seen the Father' (John 14:9)...After these plain declarations by Jesus Christ, can any one who professes to believe in Him, think it safe to approach to, or worship, or call upon any other being but Him? Or rather must it not be evident to every considerate of the Sacred Writings, that Jesus Christ is the Only proper object of Christian adoration, and that whosoever approaches unto Him, approaches at the same time unto ALL THE FULNESS OF THE GODHEAD BODILY (Col. 2:9).

"The mistake therefore of those who, in their addresses to heaven, do not go immediately to Jesus Christ, but to some other Being, whom they call the Father, appears to lie there. They consider the Father out of, and separate from, Jesus Christ, instead of believing and acknowledging what the Scriptures testify, that the Father is in Jesus Christ, and One with Him. For did all Christians really see and confess this great Gospel truth, that the Eternal Father, called in the Old Testament Jehovah, dwelleth with all His fulness in the Son, and is One with Him, it would seem impossible for them to think of approaching to, or finding, the Father out of and separate from the Son, but they would be convinced to their inexpressible comfort, that in approaching to the Son, or Divine Humanity, that they must of necessity approach to and find the Father."

And finally from page 460—"Let us then again imagine that we hear Jesus Christ ask: 'Do you see that ALL THE FULNESS of the Everlasting Father dwells bodily in Me, so that I and My Father are one?...Do you see therefore, that it is in vain for you to think of finding rest unto your souls until you come unto Me, your manifested, visible, and approachable God, in Whom the unmanifested, invisible, and unapproachable is made known and brought nigh unto you; for he that seeth Me seeth the Father, and therefore by Me, if any man enter in, he shall go in and out and find pasture.' "

The book from which we have been quoting was dedicated to the congregation of St. John's Church in Manchester, England. That such a masterpiece of Scriptural Truth would be preserved and later discovered in an abandoned church proves the importance God places on the preaching of His Word. All we can say is—"To God be the glory!"

Made in the USA
Columbia, SC
30 August 2017